SHAKING THE TREE

Vol. 6

brazen. short. memoir.

WHAT

JUST

HAPPENED?

EDITED BY
MARNI FREEDMAN & TRACY J. JONES

GET THE WHOLE COLLECTION

Memoir Writers Press is an imprint of IMWA
3639 Midway Drive, Ste. B-198
San Diego, CA 92110-5254
InternationalMemoirWriters.org

This book is a memoir anthology. It reflects the authors' present recollections of experiences over time. Some names and characteristics have been changed, some events may have been compressed, and dialogue may be recreated.

Copyedited by Erin Willard
Proofread by Tracy J. Jones
Book cover and interior design by Caroline Gilman

First edition Library of Congress Control Number: available upon request.

ISBN (paperback): 979-8-218-56350-9

WHAT JUST HAPPENED?

Acknowledgements is made to the following, in which the stories in this Anthology first appear, some differently titled or in different form:

Andrews, Hannah. "Classic Vinyl: How a Former Rock Goddess Unlocked the Mystery of My Past." *Human Parts*. Medium. September 12, 2023. https://humanparts.medium.com/classic-vinyl-966d25e8256c.

A few similar details appeared in: Esmail, Saadia Ali. "What Not to Say in an Arranged Marriage." In *Shaking the Tree: Brazen. Short. Memoir. Volume 2: Things We Don't Talk About*, edited by Marni Freedman and Tracy J. Jones, 151–156. San Diego: San Diego Memoir Writers Association, 2020.

Grey, Melissa Jordan. "A Walk in the Park." Performed at the 2022 Memoir Showcase. YouTube video. Published by San Diego Memoir Writers Association, 2022. https://youtu.be/RWhFKGCuDy0?si=g8BmMFyLQA1mYjJ2

Hager, Mahshid F. "Chaos at the Embassy." Performed at the 2022 Memoir Showcase. YouTube video. Published by San Diego Memoir Writers Association, 2022. https://www.youtube.com/watch?v=vcRWOXRnUEY.

Horton, Mary Ann. "My First Day as a Woman." Performed at the 2022 Memoir Showcase. Featuring Charles Peters. YouTube video. Published by San Diego Memoir Writers Association, 2022. https://yo utu.be/nc9Wra_fgfQ?si=yl3Nwg4NHQr6ViNg

A version of this essay was featured in Horton, Mary Ann. *Trailblazer: Lighting the Path for Transgender Equality in Corporate America.* Deerfield Beach, FL: Outskirts Press, 2022.

Hargrove, Ruth Magdi. "Saving Magdi." Performed by Melanie Mino at the 2022 Memoir Showcase. YouTube video. Published by San Diego Memoir Writers Association, 2022. https://www.youtube.com/watch?v=kYxnHlsMoJY.

Lewis, Nicole Antoinette. "Searching for My Purple." Performed by Kandance Crystal at the 2022 Memoir Showcase. YouTube video. Published by San Diego Memoir Writers Association, 2022. https://youtu.b e/4JYWxyaRFRQ?si=gMPXCiFE7LcV5gEl

Robert, Kirk. "Interview on Fifth Avenue." Performed by John Carroll at the 2022 Memoir Showcase. YouTube video. Published by San Diego Memoir Writers Association, 2022. https://youtu.be/ytDg9T ey5EI?si=B-S6GGn2-YXEe

Scoggins, K'Cee. "Forged by Steel." Performed by Katee Drysdale at the 2022 Memoir Showcase. YouTube video. Published by San Diego Memoir Writers Association, 2022. https://www.youtube.com/watch?v =45XxNRH1u6c.

Mary-Jean Zampino. "7.9 Seconds." Performed by Ruth Russell at the 2022 Memoir Showcase. Youtube video. Published by San Diego Memoir Writers Association, 2022. https://www.youtube.com/watch?v =hEzainwyEOg.

Dedicated to our writing community
who have the bravery to face the moments when life
jumps the tracks,
veers into a new reality,
and find the fierce grit to step into the unknown.

Dear Reader,

You know those times when you wake up and wonder, "How did I get here?" Whether asking hard questions or laughing at the absurdity of life's oddest curve balls, this page-turning volume will walk you through some of these soul-defining moments—unapologetically.

Raw and funny, heartbreaking and sometimes downright shocking, these stories offer insight and humor as an answer to
What
Just
Happened?

Happy reading,

Marni & Tracy

Contents

CHAOS AT THE EMBASSY

MAHSHID F. HAGER

"Turn on the TV. Turn it on now!" Dad yelled as he entered the living room. He was home early and out of breath. This was Iran in 1979.

"What now?" Mom emerged from the kitchen, still drying her hands.

I stood to greet my father. "Dad, what's going on?" The fear on his face made me lose interest in the doll I was playing with.

"Reza, are you OK? You don't look right." Mom put an instinctive protective arm around my small, eight-year-old frame. My heart began to race.

I wasn't ready for another scary event. So much had already changed in the last year. The Shah had left. Ayatollah Khomeini had taken control of the country. Since the start of the revolution, every day had been worse than the day before. So many new rules: my school became an all-girls school overnight, we all had to wear the hijab, and I wasn't allowed to play outside anymore. Mom quit her job. Music, dancing, alcohol, swimming, and sunbathing—all banned. And scarier, the violent protests, the arrests, the hangings. Fear covered the whole country in a big dark blanket. It was hard to imagine what might happen next.

We turned on the television. I saw what looked like another protest. A massive crowd was gathered, chanting "Death to America." The hatred for America and all things "Western" confused me. Before the revolution, my father traveled to Europe for work, and my whole family were big fans of American movies. But now, all of that was pure evil.

"Is that the embassy?" Mom's face turned ashen.

"What embassy?" I asked, still trying to figure out what was happening.

"The US embassy. They've been there for hours, trying to get in." Dad paced in front of the TV, not taking his eyes off the screen.

My parents had always talked about us visiting America someday. Dad had told me about the tall buildings in New York. We had friends who had been. But that was all before the revolution. I wanted to ask if we could still go, but I didn't.

The images on TV were scarier than usual, louder, and angrier. Hundreds of pro-revolution protestors were gathered, mostly men, their fists in the air, shouting and screaming, their eyes wild with rage. The feeling that something really bad was about to happen took over our whole living room.

"I can't believe they're taking it this far," Dad said. Until today, the regime's brutal crackdown had been only against Iranians, former government officials, journalists, and activists. This was their first act of violence against another nation. We watched as the protestors pushed up against the gates to the embassy. As the cameras panned out, the American flag became visible. I would probably never see New York.

"Do you think they're going to get in?" Mom asked, clearly afraid of the answer.

"Let's hope not," Dad replied, knowing that the lives of the people inside were in danger.

Protestors began shaking the gate with all their might, and while the structure rocked back and forth, it remained locked. I held my breath as I watched. I couldn't believe my eyes. Men screaming, running, and rushing the gates. No guards in sight. The familiar feeling of terror spread through my body. My limbs felt heavy; cold sweat covered my neck. I tried to be as still as possible.

"Are there still people inside?" Mom asked, as if reading my mind.

"Yes. They got ambushed. It hasn't been safe to leave. Let's hope the gate holds up."

I had a million questions and wanted to scream: *"What do they want? What will they do? Make them stop. Make them stop right now!"* But I never uttered a word. Just then, several men made it over the walls and got past the gates. Others followed. Once on the other side, the men ran toward the building.

"That's it. They're inside," Dad said, his voice trembling. "You understand, Mahin?" He grabbed Mom by the shoulders. "If they can get into the US embassy, they can get in anywhere." His words landed like a thud in my belly.

Through the worst of the protests, Mom had been saying over and over that we were safe at home. Now I felt like it was all a lie. Part of me wanted to run away and hide. That year, I had already seen more than any eight-year-old should. The images of public executions and burnt bodies were still giving me nightmares. But another part of me wanted to take in every detail, as if seeing more could somehow protect us all.

The demonstrators chanted and ran chaotically toward the building. There were cheers from the crowd as more men made their way over the gate. Within seconds, the sounds of broken glass and screams from inside the building filled the whole space.

It was like a scene from a movie: furniture and paper poured out of the embassy's windows. My heart felt like it was exploding in my chest.

One of the cameras turned and slowly zoomed in on the American flag. The men had grabbed it and were trying to rip it to shreds. I thought about my grandfather's Iranian flag; it was always handled with such care. He would bring it out only on special occasions and display it proudly in the formal living room. I was taught to treat it with respect.

We watched in disbelief as the American flag went up in flames.

"Dear God! This is not who we are. This is barbaric." Dad held his head in his hands as we watched men wave the burning flag back and forth. The crowds cheered. I was terrified of what would happen next.

"This will have consequences. We won't recover from this." Dad looked at Mom with tears in his eyes. She put a hand on his shoulder to comfort him but remained silent. I understood that whatever this event was, it would forever change how the rest of the world would view Iranians. I had grown up fast in the last couple of years. A new feeling crept up and took hold alongside fear. It was shame—though it would be decades before I could identify it. Shame for acts I didn't commit. Shame to be viewed as violent. Shame for being known as terrorists.

Demonstrators created a giant heap of office chairs, desks, paper, and filing cabinets. They poured out gasoline and set the whole thing on fire. Smoke billowed. The scene reminded me of World War II movies I had watched with my dad, and it made me choke up. I didn't want us to be known for this.

We were glued to the television well into the night, wondering, worrying, praying.

In the end, the pro-revolution militia took almost one hundred people hostage—sixty-six were Americans. They paraded the hostages out of the building, blindfolded and handcuffed.

The hostage crisis played an important role in Iran's history and clarified some things for many Iranians like my parents. Any hope that the new government would be a democratic and progressive one—concerned with Iran's standing in the world—vanished that night. The fear we felt as we watched the images stayed with us for months. "We can't stay here," Dad said to no one in particular, signaling the beginnings of an exit plan. No place was safe.

As I sat next to my mother while she wept, I thought about the family members of those hostages. They were probably watching, too, and they would be terrified. How could they not? Would they know that I was scared too? Would they know that my family and I sat around our television in Tehran and watched in horror and prayed for their loved ones? Would they know that we didn't want any of this to happen?

We watched helplessly as these same angry mobs took over our country, our towns, our neighborhoods. Our Iran, my birthplace, seemed to be slipping further and further away until it was unrecognizable. Everyone looked sad or scared all the time. You never knew when or where a brutal protest would break out. The new regime beat people on the streets, all in the name of Islam, while carrying pictures of Khomeini, the Supreme Leader. Every day, more news of people disappearing; anyone who spoke out against the regime was in danger—no one could be trusted. The streets were filled with government spies.

The hostages were released 444 days later, on January 20, 1981, but my country would never be the same. The events of that night crystallized one inevitable truth: This regime would stop at nothing to stay in power. Iran and Iranians would be isolated from the rest of the world. The regime stole my childhood, my sense of safety, and, ultimately, my home.

Nine months after the release of the hostages, my family made a heartbreaking decision to leave Iran for good. It was somewhere on the journey out of the country that I looked back and realized that my father had been right. That night set our departure in motion and changed our lives forever. We never did recover from the events of November 4, 1979.

Inconceivable

Anastasia Zadeik

I knew being on television news wasn't easy—the early, long hours and hot lights, the focus-group-selected hairstyles and practiced expressions—but I didn't realize just how hard it was until I was *actually on* television news.

The first time, several years ago, was for a live remote segment about a battle between children and seals that careened into a segment about a Spanish tourist who, while trying to stop some asshole from putting out a cigarette on the back of a seal in the Children's Pool in La Jolla, had his phone and rental car keys thrown into said Children's Pool by said asshole in what happened to be the exact spot where my kids were scheduled to complete their scuba checkout dive the next morning. When told about the tourist, the helpless seal, and the lost phone and keys, my kids offered to dive down and try to find the lost items.

I happened to be standing on the road above, watching, when the kids heroically (and rather remarkably) held the phone and keys aloft, rescuing the Spanish tourist who had rescued the seal. The Spanish tourist hugged his girlfriend. Everyone on the beach applauded. And then, the kids waved up at me, alerting a local news crew to my presence. The news crew had come to cover a protracted controversy over whether the seals should be forcibly relocated because (a) the lagoon had been given to the city for "a natural children's pool" by a wealthy woman who owned it, but (b) because of the seals, the Children's Pool regularly appeared on the list of contaminated beaches, making it dangerous for children to swim there. That morning, naturalists arguing the seals should *not* be removed had staged a protest, drawing the news crew. However, when the reporter heard about the cigarette, tourist, and key drama and saw the kids wave at me, he pivoted. "Are those your kids?" he asked. "Are you willing to answer some questions on camera?"

Full disclosure: I should have said "No" because, at the time, I knew nothing about the drama or the protracted controversy. When the reporter informed me someone had tried to put out a cigarette on a seal, I struggled to find a word that encompassed disbelief, outrage, and sorrow—and what I came up with was "inconceivable." In my defense, it was. Unfortunately, the word popped into my mind due to endless viewings of *The Princess Bride* with my kids, and it came out with a frighteningly poor imitation of the character in the movie, who says "inconceivable" repeatedly.

Recorded on a VCR tape by a friend, this was my television news legacy—for years. To this day, whenever the word "inconceivable" is uttered around me, it is done with an impression of me doing a frighteningly poor impression of Wallace Shawn.

So, when given the opportunity to record a planned segment on a Sunday morning news—one in which I would not sound like an ill-informed *Princess Bride* fangirl but rather like someone well-prepared to answer questions about the things I care about passionately (my book and the community that support-ed me in getting it published)—I was *all in.*

I prepped extensively. Watched previous Sunday morning shows. Noted segment lengths of five or six minutes. Curated my answers appropriately.

My son, who had witnessed the "inconceivable" episode on VCR multiple times, suggested I practice with him. He had this whole schtick in newscaster-y voices: "It's 72 and sunny, and I'm Tommy Tupperman with the weather. Now, back to you, Tim." Switching voices, he went on, "Good morning! I'm here with Anastasia Zadeik, author of the debut novel *Blurred Fates.*" I thanked Tim, who asked a question, which I began to answer until I suddenly heard a noise like a buzzer. "Too long," my son said. "Keep it tight." He started over with, "It's 72 and sunny . . ." We practiced for a half an hour. "Practice more," he said, as he headed to the airport.

So I did. I practiced in the shower. I practiced as I drove. I practiced as I walked the dog.

And I practiced lying in bed the night before my scheduled appearance. Having rechecked my publicist's email—"Be there at 6:45 a.m."—I'd verified the drive time—eighteen minutes—rounded up, and worked backward, allotting extra time for every step, just to be sure I wouldn't be late. Based on these calculations, I set two alarms—for 5:20 a.m. and 5:25 a.m.

When I woke up, light streamed through the windows: soft light, to be sure, but more than would be expected before 5:20 a.m. I grabbed my phone. It read 6:04 and was silently ringing because the volume had been turned down to nothing. Zero. Nada.

I scrambled out of bed and stepped into a cold shower. I rushed through an express hair wash, express make-up application, express hair drying, express coffee slugging, and express dressing. I grabbed my high heels, toothpaste, blush, and lipstick, stepped into my flip-flops, and dashed out to my trusty RAV4. I'd have time in the studio, I reasoned. Being there at 6:45 meant I'd go on at 7:15 or so, giving me time to get oriented, brush my teeth, and fix my face.

In the RAV, I pulled up the directions, began driving, and practiced. As I approached the station exit, I was "keeping it tight for a six-minute segment" when my phone rang.

It was my publicist. "Where are you?"

"Almost there," I said. "I'm going to be right on time." I was. Google Maps said I was four minutes away, and it was 6:39. I would arrive with two minutes to spare.

"Oh no. No," she said. I recognized the sound of panic. "You go ON at 6:45."

"No, no. The email said I needed to BE there at 6:45—"

"That was wrong. I was wrong. You go ON at 6:45. Can you make it?"

"I'll try," I said, thinking *I'm probably only three minutes away.* But as I hung up, distracted by the call, I drove right past the exit—right past the exit that would have given me a snowball's chance in hell of making it in time to be ON at 6:45.

"Fuck" I said, but I have to admit, I was thinking *This is inconceivable.*

Excessive speed, turning left on a red light (at an empty intersection, but still, *inconceivable*), an incorrect right turn, subsequent illegal U-turn (*inconceivable)* and my RAV4 was shrieking into the news station's empty parking lot. A man stood by a gate to my left. As I opened my door, he yelled, "Anastasia? Over here, RUN."

So I ran, in my flip-flops, saying, "I'm so sorry. I was told to BE here at 6:45."

"We'll make it work. Run," gate guy responded. "You're with Teresa."

Who's Teresa? I thought as I ran through the parking lot, where a man in a suit, maybe the weather person, added his own, "Run!" followed by an encouraging "You've got this!"

Did I have it? I thought. I clearly did not. Having it was inconceivable. I ran into the lobby, stepped out of my flip-flops, and jammed my feet into my high-heeled pumps. As I bent to pick up the flip-flops, a new guy shouted, "Leave them. This way!"

The studio was dead ahead. A real studio. Cameras, cables. Bright lights.

The new guy walked quickly toward two high stools in front of a blue wall. "Drop your bag. Phone on mute?" He didn't wait for a response. "Sit here," he said, as he grabbed a mic on a wire. "Put this on."

A beautiful blond woman with a perfect smile and bright lipstick approached. "I'm Teresa," she said. I thought about the toothbrush I'd intended to use. The lipstick. The blush.

"Can I have some water?" I said, as another guy tried to fix my mic without touching me.

"No time," he said.

Teresa hopped off her stool and took over the mic adjusting, touching me. "Sorry."

"Count to ten," someone said.

"Me?" I said.

"Yes, you. Mic check."

"1. 2. 3—"

"How long is the segment?" I asked, mentally flipping through my planned answers.

"Three minutes," Teresa said, retaking her stool. "We'll just chat. It'll be fine."

I don't have three-minute-segment answers. I asked, "Where do I look?" the word "look" faded as Teresa simultaneously said, "Good morning, San Diego." *Shit,* I thought, *Was I just asking where do I look during the intro?*

I was.

I don't remember much of the next three minutes. My son's instructions flitted through my mind. Don't touch your face. Don't fix your hair. Smile. Keep it tight. Don't talk too long. In the end, I couldn't have done the latter. The interview went by in a blur.

The whole time, I didn't know where to look.

And then, it was over. Teresa rose from her stool, holding her copy of my book, *Blurred Fates.* She held out her hand to shake mine. I rose to shake hers.

"You were great," she said.

"I was?"

Gate guy was there. "You were," he said.

I nodded, stupefied. But as I followed them both back toward my flip-flops, I couldn't help but doubt their sincerity. In fact, the idea of me "doing great" under the circumstances was, you guessed it, *inconceivable.*

My First Day as a Woman
Mary Ann Horton, PhD

As a beautiful May 1987 day drew to a close, I donned my new miniskirt and admired myself in my bathroom mirror. I didn't mind how my dark mustache looked against my long, curly brown wig. As I struck a feminine pose, I saw the headlights from my wife's car turn into our driveway. *Oh, my God.* Karen was home. She had gone to her friend's house to study—said she would be gone for the night. I snatched my pile of men's clothes from the floor and raced to the bedroom to change.

As I pulled off my blouse, I heard the front door slam. I yanked off the miniskirt as fast as I could. I heard her footsteps coming down the hall, and I crumpled the women's clothes into a ball. I pulled on my pants, kneeled on the floor to put everything in the closet, and slammed it shut. Before I could put on my shirt—Karen walked in. She looked at me, kneeling shirtless on the carpet. She gasped.

Eyeing me suspiciously, she opened the closet and looked at the crumpled pile of women's clothing. Her face read of disgust. "I come home to pick up a book, and this is what I find?" I felt a hard knot in my stomach. Without another word, she stormed out of the house.

I'd been fascinated by skirts since I was nine. I wanted to twirl. I didn't understand my compulsion to wear women's clothing. My mother beat me with a broken piece of floorboard when she discovered my collection, so I hid it in a baseball glove box. I'd tried to quit many times, but the allure was irresistible. It was an indescribable itch that I had to scratch.

I met Karen in college. I was an introverted nerd, and she was a shy girl from Ohio. We shared the same love of bleu cheese and rock music (an Elton John concert was our first date). We thought we were the perfect couple.

A few months before our wedding, I felt compelled to tell her the truth, explaining that I needed to wear women's clothing. "Oh, no, you can't do that. I knew a guy once who did that. He was weird." Neither one of us thought it was that big of a deal. I purged my collection and stayed away for two years.

The need came back when I was in grad school. Somehow, when I put on women's clothing, I felt less alone. I kept my new stash of skirts and slips hidden for three years. After graduation, all was well until the day I stepped into the living room one morning in her dress and underwear.

"So, are we ready to go?" I joked. She was not amused. My attempt to open that door to a conversation had failed. "How dare you steal my clothing." She demanded I "get counseling to get cured." I acquiesced and spent many sessions being counseled at the Open Door Clinic.

Ex-gay therapy doesn't work, and neither does ex-trans therapy. For two years, I was able to resist my compulsion by reminding myself how important my wife was to me.

From the outside, we looked like the typical suburban family—two kids, two Honda hatchbacks, and a house with a large backyard. Karen was a stay-at-home mom, and I was an engaged dad.

In between family dinners and changing diapers, I began to collect a new stash. After Karen went to bed, I was unable to resist temptation. Around this time, Karen's focus shifted. She withdrew emotionally, and the "I love yous" stopped.

My wife's discovery crushed me. Now, she had no doubt I'd been cross-dressing in her absence, and I knew she would not keep it a secret. As days went by, a cloud of shame hung over our house. Her family visibly recoiled when they saw me. They knew.

I checked in with Karen. "Are you okay? You've barely spoken to me."

"I'm deciding if I want a divorce."

I didn't want a divorce. I wanted my family, my wife back, the person who calmed me down and hugged me like no one else. My cravings to cross-dress were about to upend my life. *There must be something terribly wrong with me. Why do I have this burning desire to cross-dress? Am I some kind of pervert?* I wrestled with this soul-torturing question.

Over the years, I'd worn nylons under my male clothes, but that was it. I wondered what it would be like to spend an entire day where I fully presented as a woman. I feared I'd find out I loved it.

A few weeks later, when traveling to Arizona for a conference, I found an unexpected opportunity. I could skip the first day and spend it as a woman. One big problem—my mustache. If I shaved, this action would be the point of no return. My naked face would tell Karen what I'd done. Our marriage would be over.

I packed my thirty-dollar Kmart wig and a pair of size 13 pumps and headed to the conference. That morning, I turned on my electric shaver and went for it. My face looked naked, and my heart pounded. I drove to the nearest mall. My first stop was Montgomery Ward for ladies' underwear. I picked out a bra, panties, and black tights and hoped I had the right size. I felt relief when the teenage checkout clerk rang up my purchases without a reaction.

My next stop, The Limited, would have a good selection of women's clothing. As I browsed the long denim skirts, a twenty-ish saleswoman approached.

"What size are you looking for?"

"I don't know . . . a-about my size?"

She selected a size 16 skirt and a matching denim shirt. I had no idea how they would fit, and I didn't want to go back to the hotel to try them on. *Well*, I thought, *I guess it's do or die.* I summoned my courage. "These are for me. May I try them on?"

She contorted her face. *Is it against the law for me to use a ladies' fitting room?* She looked around the empty store and picked up her key.

Everything fit. Still a bundle of nerves, I put my men's clothes back on and paid. Then, I had a new problem. How would I change into my women's clothes for the rest of my day? I couldn't use either mall restroom for a gender change. Shedding my last bit of masculinity, I asked, "I'd like to wear them out of the store. May I use your dressing room again?" She let me back in.

I had brought along extra socks and used them to pad my bra. Black tights covered my hairy legs. I adjusted my wig. I stared at the mirror, seeing myself in a complete female presentation. I smiled, my eyes agog. This felt right. I made a beeline for the exit.

I stepped into the mall, which was teeming with retirees. I felt their icy stares as they sized me up, an ungainly six-footer wearing a denim shirt and long skirt, black tights, high heels, and a cheap wig. A little makeup would help. At the far end of the mall, I spotted a hippie-style boutique. I pushed aside a beaded curtain. A sweet lady offered me my first smile and invited me in.

"We can do a makeover for twenty-five dollars. That okay?"

I didn't know what a makeover was, but I was game. "Sure."

"My name is Stacy. What's yours?"

Until that moment, it had never occurred to me that "Mark" wasn't the right answer. I had no idea what to say. In a moment of inspiration, I blurted, "My name is Mary Ann." I always liked Dawn Wells from *Gilligan's Island.*

Over the next two hours, she worked on my face. We chatted as she brushed along my eyelids. I liked how it felt. Stacy had a gentle touch. When we were done, I was amazed by my reflection—while I was no beauty queen, a pleasant female face smiled back at me. I looked nice.

Stopping by Woolworths for a purse, lipstick, and wallet, I noticed most of the stares had disappeared among the walking crowd.

I drove to a Wendy's drive-through and ordered lunch at the speaker. The clerk thanked me and called me "sir." I cringed. I pulled up, and when he saw my female face, he looked confused.

For the remainder of the day, I worked on my book in a beautiful public park. I went to a nice restaurant for dinner and saw a movie. I felt more comfortable than I had in months. Back at the hotel, I rushed to my room to avoid being seen. I washed off my makeup, put my male clothes back on, and reflected on the day. How did it feel to be Mary Ann? Was it as exhilarating as I expected?

The word that came to mind was "boring." It wasn't the rush I'd expected. I just felt relaxed. Is that the life I wanted?

But thoughts of my two little ones, Sunday morning pancakes, and reading Dr. Seuss at bedtime called to me. So, I took all my female clothes, including the wig and heels, and threw them into the trash. I resolved not to cross-dress anymore. My family was more important to me. After the conference ended, I flew back to face Karen and to resume my life as Mark.

This time on the plane, a new question taunted me. "Who am I, really?"

Janet vs. Goliath

Janet Hafner

"Too many tests. Too expensive. Unnecessary."

It sounds like a case of three strikes, and you're out. The back of my neck tingled. My blood pressure skyrocketed.

"You insurance companies are all alike. You deny everyone's claim if you can get away with it.

"Twelve doctors couldn't tell me why I have no equilibrium, why my joints are on fire twenty-four seven, or why I don't sleep. It's bullshit."

"It doesn't—" she began. I cut her off.

"I found a doctor whose thinking and treatments are unconventional. He knows what's wrong with me, but he needs those test results for confirmation."

"I can't—" she sputtered.

"You listen to me. I got prior approval from your office before I had the tests. Now you're trying to tell me that you're not going to cover these tests?" I hammered out the words. "More bullshit. Get your supervisor. I want to—" She interrupted me.

"I know you've called several times, and the answer is the same. Can't change it."

"Get me the person who can." Before I got an answer, she hung up. My cheeks burned. My body was tight.

"I'm guessing they won't pay the three thousand dollars the tests cost." My husband's face showed his disgust. "What's your next move?"

My voice was hard. "I need to take charge of this situation. If I can't get the insurance company to pay as they said they would, I'll . . . I'll take them to small claims court. I'll sue their sorry . . ." My heart thumped as blood was replaced with an unfamiliar, scary determination. It swept through me. I stood taller.

"Are you going to hire an attorney?" My husband's voice was serious.

"Noooooooooo." I dragged out the word with all the air I had in my lungs. "I'm going to represent myself. I don't have experience, but I've got to do it."

As his arms wrapped around my tense body, he chuckled and whispered in my ear, "This is a case of David and Goliath, but this time it's Janet and Goliath."

I waited in the Vista Superior Courthouse, wearing a crisp white blouse, black slacks, a charcoal jacket, best black pumps, and silver earrings—my version of what a lawyer might wear. I didn't have a briefcase. Instead, I carried a manila folder guarding a two-inch stack of medical records, denial letters, and a detailed letter from Dr. Leshenko.

For over a year, I'd suffered. My joints on fire, insomnia, no equilibrium, ringing in my ears. The problem was I looked healthy, but I was sick. Really sick. Twelve doctors. I got nothing more than a referral to a psychiatrist. Dr. Leshenko was the last name on the list of doctors who might know what was going on. My last hope.

My husband sat next to me in the bright hallway outside Courtroom 3. The heat of his leg warmed my icy body. Across the hallway stood three utterly professional-looking lawyers. *They're here to defend the insurance company,* I thought.

They whispered. They shot glances my way. Each carried a worn leather briefcase. Two brown, one black. When the clerk opened the dark oak double doors, they rushed in and occupied the front row. We filed into the fourth row on the left. *Damn, I'm an army of one, and the insurance company sent three.* I wiped my sweaty palms on my slacks. I closed my eyes and traced the air as it traveled in and out of my lungs.

My husband bent toward me and whispered, "This is small claims court. No jury, no deliberation in chambers. After the judge listens to both sides, he'll give his ruling. We won't have to wait."

You've got to do a good job. A lot is riding on it.

I thought back to my first meeting with Dr. Leshenko. A man with disheveled salt-and-pepper hair and an unconventional approach. He was a wobbly six-foot figure who hobbled into the room on a left foot wrapped with Ace bandages. He carried a beat-up brown leather briefcase dangling at his side, with papers sticking out from under the lock. A chill shook me. The VA hospital spokesperson had told me, "He's the one to see when no one else can find the problem."

Crystal-clear icy blue eyes studied me. Turning his attention to his blank yellow notepad, he hesitated a moment and then said, "Tell me everything."

I rattled off my symptoms.

"I think I know what's causing your problems." *He can help me.*

He riffled through papers in his old briefcase; then, he snapped it shut.

"You have to go to two different specialty labs in Los Angeles for a series of tests. The only way to confirm what I suspect is with these tests.

"Tests first, then we'll talk. How soon can you get your lab work done?"

"This week."

"Blah, blah, blah and blah, blah, blah." I looked up. *I heard my case number.*

Three attorneys, in unison, stood. Papers in hand. One by one, they presented their documentation—the evidence to prove their case against me. I'd heard it all before in the denial correspondence. Too expensive. Too many. Unnecessary. I watched the judge. His eyes watched each attorney as he spoke. When they finished, one asked if he could approach the bench. I couldn't hear what he said. My heart raced. The lawyer handed a thick folder to the judge. My husband rested his hand on my leg. *Stay calm,* I reminded myself. One attorney looked at me. His tight lips morphed into a smirk.

The presiding judge was old enough to be my grandfather. His eyes scanned the courtroom. His baritone voice asked, "Is the attorney who is representing the plaintiff in the courtroom?" The room was still. I knew from Judge Judy that if someone didn't come forward, the case was dismissed, so I waved at the judge, found my feet, and stood. My lips parted just enough for sounds to escape, but no words left my mouth.

"Ms. Hafner, am I to understand that you are representing yourself?" He stared with deep-set eyes. My mouth was dry. Tongue stuck to the roof of my mouth. The judge cleared his throat.

I dug deep, and when I found it, my voice popped out. "Your Honor, I'm here to represent myself in this lawsuit against the Consortium Health Care Program."

I could swear the judge's lips fought a smile. "Are you ready to present your case?"

"I am, Your Honor," I said, without my voice splintering into shards.

The judge stared. Finally, he asked, "Do you have anything you'd like me to review?"

"Yes, Your Honor." My right hand holding the evidence trembled, and by the time I stood before the judge, it was a full-on earthquake. The bailiff took my folder. I sat down. *It's all up to the judge now.* The first document in the folder was the all-important letter. He read and reread each page, then reviewed the lab reports and the rejection letters and gave everything a third reading.

"So, Mrs. Hafner, it appears you've been very ill with an auto-immune disease, Mycoplasma fermentans." He paused to study me.

"Yes, Your Honor," I barely whispered.

My ears strained to hear the judge's words while every muscle in my chest tensed. Anxiety took over.

Suddenly, short, sharp sounds erupted from my gut. "I got prior approval and now the insurance company won't pay. It's just not right, Your Honor."

Be quiet. You shouldn't have talked out of turn. I lowered my head. Tears pooled, but I didn't let them fall.

The judge scowled over his black-rimmed glasses at the defense attorneys. He asked, "Does the defense have anything else they wish to say?"

"No, Your Honor."

In the seconds of silence, the judge rearranged all the papers before him. As he finished, he looked at the attorneys, and then his eyes settled on me.

I closed my eyes. My shoulders rose with an incoming breath.

I did the best I could. I'm not a lawyer. I shouldn't have spoken like that. They're going to get away with it.

The judge's "ah-hem" registered in my ears, causing my eyelids to flutter.

"After careful consideration, I have determined that the plaintiff has provided sufficient evidence that the tests in question were necessary and not excessive. I, therefore, rule in favor of the plaintiff. All present and future medical bills related to these conditions as set forth by the plaintiff are to be paid without delay."

The words skipped through my brain as I listened. Not sure what I had heard, I turned to my husband. "What. Just. Happened?"

"You beat Goliath, honey. You won. You kicked their butts."

Everything I Was Doing Was Wrong

Jocelyn Hough

I slept by the front door for weeks so my dad couldn't walk out of the house at 4 a.m. I slept lightly, like someone who'd been traumatized by a burglar. *Oh, God.* There's that creaking sound. He's creeping down the stairs, and I'm sick to my stomach because I know what's about to happen. *How am I going to stop him this time?* Whatever I say is going to start a battle. But I have to try to bring him back to reality somehow.

"Where you headed?"

"None of your beeswax."

He attempted to open the front door but struggled with the deadbolt. "Open the goddamn door!"

"But you're dressed in pajamas and a suit coat."

"I have to get downtown to argue a case before the Supreme Court."

"But it's 4 a.m., and you retired from your law practice ten years ago."

"You're lying."

"Plus, the Supreme Court is in DC, and we're in San Diego."

He gave me a condescending smirk. "Go to hell."

I blocked the door with my body, but he shoved me out of the way.

"I'm gonna have to call 911 for your own safety if you walk out that door."

That stopped him in his tracks. I thought I'd gotten through to him, but he turned around and gave me a look of utter hatred. This was not my dad—we were two peas in a pod. Baseball games, museums, watching *America's Funniest Videos,* and eating vanilla ice cream. But not today.

"If you call 911, I'll sue you." Then he gave me the finger and headed toward the sidewalk.

I peppered him with logic. "How are you going to get downtown? Why are you in your pajamas? If you're in Washington, why are there palm trees everywhere?" All that did was piss him off. That's because, as it turns out, *everything I was doing was wrong.*

He continued down the darkened sidewalk. I knew better than to grab his arm, because that made him aggressive, but I couldn't let him wander into traffic. I was at my wits' end. These middle-of-the-night shenanigans had been going on for weeks. I called my brother, Tommy, who arrived within minutes. He pulled alongside our dad.

"Hey, Pop, I heard you were out for an early morning walk."

Furious, he barked, "Did she tell you to come get me?"

"She was worried about you. So am I. C'mon, get in the car, and I'll drive us back to the house." Amazingly, my dad got in the car, and off they went down the street. By the time I got there, they were sitting on the couch with the TV on, laughing and chatting.

LET'S CALL IT COGNITIVE DECLINE

Tommy and I made an appointment for our dad to see a neurologist. Our dad didn't understand what all the fuss was about. A nurse took him to do some cognition tests so we could talk. "Is it Alzheimer's?" I asked.

"Well, we won't know for sure until he dies and we look at his brain. If you let us."

Sheesh. Bedside manner much?

She continued, "There's no test that definitively says 'Alzheimer's.' That said, he does seem to have a number of markers for Alzheimer's. But let's just call it 'cognitive decline.'"

I jumped in. "Oh, he is *way* beyond cognitive decline. And if it is Alzheimer's, I need to know what to do or what to expect."

She told me to expect some physical changes. "His legs can become weak; he may fall a lot; he may choke on his food and inhale his saliva." No mention that he might become paranoid or accuse me of holding him hostage.

"Where are my goddamn keys?!" It was only a couple of days after the doctor, and he was frantically searching the house.

I tried to remain calm. "When's the last time you used your keys? Did you check your coat pocket?"

But when my father turned to answer me, a stranger with evil eyes whispered, "C'mon, Jocie. I know you took them."

"No, Dad, I promise you, I didn't take them. I don't know where they are, but I'll help you look for them."

And then the evil man spoke with the Scottish brogue of his parents: "Aye Jocie, ye know ye took 'em. I'm onto you."

I was stunned. Who is this stranger? Tears welled up. I couldn't get any words out.

Pleased that I was upset, he laughed. "I *got* ye."

BASICALLY, YOU HAVE TO LIE

It had been a year since my dad's Alzheimer's non-diagnosis. His neurologist never used the word "Alzheimer's," even when my dad asked flat-out if that's what he had. But we all knew—even my dad. I privately asked her why she wouldn't use the word. She said there was no reason to.

And then I witnessed a moment that changed everything. In the waiting room, I noticed a patient refusing to go home because he didn't know where his wife was. A nurse told him, "Your wife had to run an errand, and she asked your son-in-law to take you home." The man was instantly relieved, and the son-in-law was able to wheel him away. The nurse looked at me and said, "The wife has been dead for years."

I was incredulous. "Why not say, compassionately, that his wife had passed away but that the son-in-law was right here to take him home?"

She smiled and said five magical words: "Basically, you have to lie."

"So, when the man gets home, and the wife isn't there, won't he realize he was duped and become angry?"

"He won't even remember what was said by the time he gets to the elevator."

"So every time he gets anxious about his wife's whereabouts—"

"They usually say she's at the store. All he needs is an answer to get out of the loop in his head." It felt cruel to me, as if they were making fun of him. But, as I would soon learn, it really does take away their anxiety. Just to get an answer. Any answer.

Our dad's condition was deteriorating, and reluctantly, I had to acknowledge that I was no longer able to provide the care he needed. So his doctor recommended that my brother and I move him into what's called a "memory-care facility." It's for people in the early stages of Alzheimer's. We were fortunate to find our dad a brand-new memory-care facility. The residents all had their own private rooms, but with doors that didn't lock. The rooms entered into a beautiful multi-purpose area complete with a gourmet kitchen, a library, a gym, and a pool. Our dad had one of the larger rooms, with a big-screen TV and windows that looked out onto lush gardens. Beyond the gardens were locked courtyards. The day we moved our dad into the facility, my dad put on his coat to leave with us. My brother stopped him. "Oh, you don't have to put your coat on, Pop. You live *here* now. This is your new home."

"I don't live here. I live at home, and I want to go back home now!"

He didn't understand. Absolutely broke my heart. Holding back tears, we told him, "You *are* home. This is your new home. This is your new apartment."

He shoved me and other staffers out of the way in defiance, trying to get to a door. "I don't live here!"

I thought about what the nurse had said, so I blurted out, "We'll be going home shortly!" This did indeed stop him in his tracks.

He said, "When?" Crap. I wasn't used to lying to my dad. I had to buy time to think of what to say next.

My brother jumped in. "The nurse said we have to fill out a few forms before we leave."

My dad grew suspicious. "What are the forms for?"

I could see my brother struggling, "Um . . . insurance forms?"

"Insurance for what?"

Neither my brother nor I answered quickly enough. "Insurance for what?!? And how long is this going to take?"

I tried to stall. "Uh . . . maybe, like, twenty minutes."

My dad became agitated again. "I'm not going to wait twenty minutes! I want to go home now. Don't worry about the goddamn forms!"

A staffer overheard us and took pity. "I'll take your daughter to sign the forms right now." Amazingly, my dad became calm. The staffer pulled me aside. "You need to be vague. Never give specifics, or you'll end up in a loop." *Okay. Lie and be vague.*

It took a while to get the hang of it. One time, during a visit, my dad asked where my mother was, and I forgot to lie. "Gosh, Dad, remember, Mom passed away seven years ago."

That set him off. "You're a liar! Why are you lying?"

A nearby staffer jumped in to save me. "Didn't you tell us your mother was meeting her girlfriends for lunch?"

"Oh, that's right. Sorry, Dad, I forgot. She's having lunch with her girlfriends."

He always had a follow-up. "How long will she be?"

This time, I was ready. "Y'know, she didn't say. Could be a long time, though. You know how they get when they're all together!" I faked a laugh, and then he laughed. It worked! I told him that lie every time he asked where my mother was. He never remembered having heard it before. Lying made all the difference—lies gave him peace. And that's all I wanted for him.

Interview on Fifth Avenue

Robert Kirk

I t was 1991, my first year away at college in New York City, and I needed a job. I was twenty years old, finally living away from home. After two rehabs, I was newly sober yet again. I wasn't destitute, but I wanted to show my parents that I could be a productive, working member of society. It was time to get a real job.

I looked through the Help Wanted ads. One ad in the *Village Voice* caught my eye. It was from a Midtown art dealer looking for an office assistant.

Working in the New York art world? That sounded perfect. Art, literature, entertainment—that's what New York was all about.

I called and spoke to the man, Mr. Rivington. He greeted me in this deep, gravelly voice and asked a few basic questions. When he figured out I was a college student from San Diego, he wanted to meet me right away. I guessed maybe he was an art dealer intrigued by all things California.

"Let's talk in person some night this week after you're done with school," he said.

Score! I had an interview for a prestigious and legit job.

Mr. Rivington ran his business from home. The interview would be at his Fifth Avenue apartment.

A few evenings later, I headed uptown, a little nervous, but excited. My mind raced with images of working with somebody like Andy Warhol, going to superstar-filled parties, and pop art everywhere. I walked through the revolving door of the 1960s-style brick building into a lobby that felt like a fancy hotel, with marble floors, polished wood trim, white couches. It was Manhattan rich, the real deal. I instantly knew I wanted the job. I had to play this interview right.

I walked over to the uniformed man behind a concierge desk. "I'm here to see Mr. Rivington in 1501."

The desk man picked up the phone and called Mr. Rivington.

"You may go up," he said with a strange smirk, nodding toward the four sleek elevators.

I rode up, and when I stepped into the fifteenth-floor hallway, my feet sank into the lush carpet. I looked around at the crystal sconce lighting and white crown molding.

At Unit 1501, I pushed the door open slightly, giving a knock. Mr. Rivington had told me to walk right in, but I felt weird. What if I was at the wrong place?

"Come in," I heard the same gravelly voice from the phone shout out.

I closed the door and stepped into the foyer. It opened into a massive corner living room. Everything was dark except for the sparkling city lights streaming in through all the windows. The view looked straight down Fifth Avenue to Washington Square Park.

"I'm in the bedroom."

I saw a light coming from an open door at the end of the hall. Strange, but I figured a psycho wouldn't live in an apartment this expensive. And truthfully, I'd wandered into much sketchier places to buy meth.

When I got to the bedroom, I saw Mr. Rivington lying in bed, covered in a sheet, apparently naked and ready for the interview. He was a large man. The bed was solid, with a thick wood frame, but his body sank deep into a sagging middle section of the bed. He was bald, with puffs of brownish gray at the sides.

"Hello, please, have a seat," he said, motioning me to a wooden chair next to the bed.

Okay. Yes, I was surprised he was naked and in bed for the job interview. That was unexpected. But I quickly assessed the situation. I could work with a scene like this. I knew what I brought to the table in situations like this. Youth. I'd met plenty of older men who liked having people my age around. Older guys just got happy being around an attentive youth. I could be the innocent college kid this art dealer wanted to hire.

Mr. Rivington explained that he bought and sold contemporary works of art from around the world and needed an assistant to help keep up with the paperwork. I'd be answering the phone, sorting bills, filing invoices, those sorts of things.

"We'll start the pay at $10 an hour. But if it's a good fit, I'll increase that in a few months."

The minimum wage was $4.25 at the time, so ten dollars an hour was nice. He seemed impressed that I studied liberal arts at the New School. He also wanted to know if I surfed and liked hanging out shirtless at the beach back home in San Diego.

"I think you'd be ideal for this position," he finally said, after we'd chatted a while.

A jolt of excitement raced through me. I did it. I had a real New York job.

"Wow, thank you. This is perfect. Thank you, sir."

I sat there imagining parties at the Met. Openings at MOMA. Cab rides, or maybe even limo rides to Soho galleries. I felt a surge of pride. My parents would be thrilled.

I stood up to leave.

"Oh, one more thing," he said.

I sat back down.

"I'm also going to need you to wash my testicles."

What?

Did he just say what I think he said?

"I've gained so much weight that I can't reach them."

A visual of this particular problem passed through my mind. What exactly would he be needing me to do? I wasn't sure what to say.

"But that's all. I won't need any other personal assistance."

"I don't know," I said.

We were both silent.

"I mean, I want the job, thank you," I said, not wanting to blow it. "But I'll need to think this testicle part over."

"I understand, you think about it and give me a call in the next day or two and let me know what you decide."

I thanked him for his time and left. The concierge in the lobby gave me a sly grin. I wondered if perhaps watching young guys come and go from Mr. Rivington's apartment was a routine thing.

I got back to my dorm room and called my new AA sponsor, Danny, to see what he'd suggest. Danny was older, about thirty, born and raised in Queens. He was definitely smart about these things. He'd know what to do. Ten dollars an hour and a job with an art dealer sounded good.

"This doesn't sound good," Danny said, without much hesitation.

"It was a sweet apartment."

"If he needs help washing his balls, then he needs to hire a nurse, not a young office assistant."

I thought about what Danny said. He was right. I was not a nurse.

I telephoned Mr. Rivington.

"I'd like the job."

"Wonderful."

"But I don't think I can wash your testicles for ten dollars an hour."

"You make a good point," Mr. Rivington said. "Why don't we track the time and do sixty dollars an hour for that? Then we'll do ten dollars an hour for everything else."

Sixty dollars an hour was a boatload of money. I could basically skip the subway and always do cabs, and I could drink as many Diet Cokes as I wanted at the Limelight.

"That's very generous of you, sir," I said, imagining the size of those paychecks.

No, stand firm. I am a sober, responsible, legitimate adult.

"But I really don't want to do that part at all."

"Oh. That's too bad. It is a requirement of the job."

I was disappointed as we hung up. I looked out my dorm room window at the towers of Lower Manhattan, my dream city. I'd finally arrived. I had no issue being the young guy adding a little nostalgia to an older man's scene. But I knew I'd made the right decision. Mr. Rivington's job requirement veered into hustling, and honestly, for hustling work, sixty dollars an hour wasn't really all that great. Besides, what would I have told my parents? Your sober son is now a Midtown testicle scrubber?

Soon after that, I started working at Blockbuster Video in Greenwich Village, which didn't quite pay ten dollars an hour, but it did land me a real job smack in the middle of the world's most legendary artist neighborhood. My perks included free video rentals, movie star customers, and lots of eccentric characters for a writer like me to observe. Every night, I chatted with a parade of West Village film buffs, many of whom probably would have jumped all over that job offer of washing Mr. Rivington's balls.

This happened more than thirty years ago. I'm still sober, and Danny is still my sponsor. I shared this story with him recently. His reply?

"You never told me he offered you sixty dollars an hour. If I'd known that, I might have given you different advice."

Adapt and Thrive

Nancy L. O'Sullivan

Words flew from Stacey's mouth as soon as she rounded the corner of our house. "You guys, Tess had a spitting cobra in her house!" Mike stood so quickly that his three-legged stool flew almost to the door.

"What?! Did it bite her? Did it spit? Is she okay?" Our words tangled and merged.

"No bites, no blindness, no death. Apparently, Tess already knew cobras would try to spit venom into your eyes. It took an hour, but she managed to escape her house and avoid the snake, all while holding her hands between her eyes and the cobra."

"Oh, my god." I sat back down. "When was this? How is she?"

"Three days ago. Tess is pretty tough, but she lives alone. She's staying with Tina now."

Mike, Stacy, and I exchanged glances, but none of us spoke for a moment. It was 1987. We were Peace Corps volunteers in our twenties in the Central African Republic. We did not have local healthcare, running water, electricity, or phones. "Adapt and thrive" was a common phrase thrown out at our trainings. "You'll make it work." We had made it work so far, but unease about the distance between us and health care crept up and through me. If I found a dangerous animal in my home, would I be able to handle it?

Stacey turned to go. "I just stopped by to give you Tess's news and collect outgoing mail." Mike turned toward the house. I stood and stared at the muddy river flowing fifty feet in front of me.

Mike gave Stacey letters for our families and friends. Would my next letter home relate Tess's story? No. They'd worry. What would they think if Mike or I never came home?

As Stacey's motorcycle sputtered to life, the sky darkened into evening lavender and smoky grays. Mike stood close to me and took my hand. We silently watched the river swirl and eddy. A small bird swooped down and across our view, then another, then a cluster. Back and forth, they dove and turned. The hair on the back of my neck rose. They were not birds. They were bats.

Bats could carry rabies.

I wrapped my arms tightly around my chest. "I'm going inside."

"They're just bats," Mike said, his rational brain in charge. "They eat insects. They're not doing anything to us."

"Mm-hmm," I answered, tucking my head down and lunging toward the house.

The cloud of bats thickened and swooped low with apparent purpose. In three large steps, Mike crossed the yard. "They're coming from under the roof," he shouted indignantly. "They live in our house." As we slammed the wooden door shut, the house darkened, lit only by the last light of the day filtering in between wooden window slats. Mike lit our kerosene lamp. The house held a dozen bats, the color of dusk, mice with wings.

I grabbed a broom and flashlight and banged my elbow hard on the cement wall. Pain sizzled. Anger rose. Protests swarmed in my head. I had taken an entire panel of vaccines to stay healthy in this country. I took anti-malarial pills every day. I had survived mystery viruses and intestinal upsets. I was not in the mood for rabies and a slow, painful death. Broom in hand, I circled our wooden table, avoiding the lamp and swatting the air. Ordinarily compassionate, I felt victorious when my broom made contact with a bat.

I ventured into our bedroom. A bat flew in between the louvers of one window and out another. Several circled overhead. Their shadows spiraled like a funeral kaleidoscope. Fear rose ever higher in the claustrophobic space. I ducked down and swayed an awkward dance of avoidance. A bat rustled my hair. I inhaled through clenched teeth, barricading my throat and lungs. My thoughts focused: I must do anything, everything, to be safe.

"The net," I yelled, though Mike stood next to me. With trembling hands, I helped unroll the gauzy mosquito net that hung from the ceiling above our mattress. I clumsily climbed onto the mattress, hugged my knees, and listened to the rapid thudding of my heart. Mike tucked the mosquito net in after him and gave me a quick sideways hug. Hot and sweaty, we sat side by side. I did not remember when I last felt fear this way. And betrayal. Others occupied this house, and they had just attacked us.

Mike stroked my hair. I wanted to smile and say I was fine. He waited. I wanted to be stronger than fear, but it gripped me—fierce and jittery.

"When the bat got in my hair, I thought I was done for," I managed.

"It raised my pulse a bit, too. We'll be okay. The bats want to get out as much as we want them out."

"Not that one," I said, pointing to the small gray mass clinging to the netting above our heads. Mike took off his shoe and bunted it off the netting.

"Home run!" he said, with a grin. I tried to smile but couldn't. "We'll plug the hole the bats are using to enter the attic," Mike added, in a comforting voice. "They'll relocate."

Staying low to the floor, Mike fully opened the louvers on the bedroom windows. Several bats flew out the river-facing window. I sat, still hugging my knees, watching the ceiling for shadows and the room's corners for movement.

When all was apparently quiet, we ventured outside. I carried the broom and flashlight with me. The bats were gone, but I couldn't shake the feeling that the way things had gone, it was probably the day a deadly snake would show up in the pit toilet behind the house. Or the pit would collapse. Mike and I inspected the area together. I finished my business quickly and stood guard for Mike. With uneven breath, I reentered the house, checked carefully that the mosquito netting was secured around the mattress, and willed myself into a solid, dreamless sleep.

At 5:24 a.m., the sky was light. People talked and called to each other along the riverbank. The past evening's events seemed surreal. The only evidence was the abundance of grass seeds and twigs that were once part of the broom. I stepped out from under the netting onto the warm and solid concrete floor.

Mike passed the open doorway with the stiff little body of a bat we hit last night. "Found two," he said, "I wanted to get them out before you woke up."

I tried to pretend that didn't happen. It was too early in the day for dead things in the house, too early for bat adventures. Coffee would be next. I picked up pants from the bedroom chair and pulled the first leg up. It felt tight, as if socks were inside. I slid my hand down the leg to pull them out. There was a soft, squishy, hand-sized mound in the pant leg that was definitely not socks. In one quick twitch, my pants were on the floor, my hand in the air, and I was halfway through the doorway to the main room, exhaling a short, high "Ahhhhhhk!" as I went. I inhaled quickly and leaned over as if lightheaded.

"What?" Mike asked, rushing in with deep concern. I was silent for a moment, then began to laugh, in short bursts at first, then deeper. As I rose to stand, the laugh became an uncontrollable stream, rolling through me and soaring out my mouth. My eyes watered, and I was fighting for breath.

I touched it. I touched a bat. In my pants. And lived to tell about it.

Tess was not bitten. She was not blinded. She figured out what to do.

Mike and I were not bitten or scratched. We defended ourselves.

We'll patch the hole into the attic. Bats will relocate.

We can do it. Adapt and thrive.

As one should. As I will.

A WALK IN THE PARK

MELISSA JORDAN GREY

Somewhere in the assembly process, God forgot my neck. Crewnecks fit like turtlenecks, and turtlenecks come up to my chin. God failed to give me a button nose, too. It's more like a proboscis. A perfect word, prrrrrrrro-bosssssssscis. Long, unwieldy, and uncouth. Kind of like the boyfriend who once told me, "You're not fat. You're just . . . dense." Like my nose, apparently.

Sensing my lack of beauty and poise, my stepmother enrolled me in the Park Seven modeling school when I was thirteen. "What a wonderful opportunity to learn to be ladylike," she said. But I already knew what was wrong with me. Why pay someone to point it out?

Half modeling agency, half charm school, Park Seven stood in a nondescript cinderblock building wedged between a Chevron and a Taco Bell. A foul mix of refried beans and gas fumes greeted every Christie Brinkley wannabe who entered. It greeted me, too.

Park Seven required its "ladies" to come in heels, so I pulled my JC Penny cork-soled platform sandals out of the box and onto my feet at the last minute. But even heels didn't help me much. Picture all four-foot-ten of me among towering blondes named Brittany, Tiffany, and Harper. I didn't stand a chance.

Every dreaded Monday, at the start of each class, Miss Estelle Clapp would ask, "Now, ladies, tell me your Park Seven dream."

"To be on the cover of *Vogue*," said one of the Brittanies.

"To be a runway model," said one of the Tiffanies.

"To be the next Cindy Crawford," said a Harper.

Then, inevitably, Miss Clapp would point to me.

"To be the best jazz saxophonist in the country," I declared, each and every time.

I loved jazz—its soaring, unbound tangents and outside-the-lines melodies. While the other girls cooed over Duran Duran, I fantasized about trading fours with Charlie Parker. But apparently, I didn't look like that part either. The day I brought my horn to school, the comments began:

"Girls don't play the saxophone."

"What boy will like you now?"

"Why don't you play the flute, Lila? It's so much more ladylike."

Miss Clapp didn't get me any more than they did. "Jazz saxophone?!" she sneered, as a nervous hush fell over the room. Mortified, I wanted to dig my Lee Press-On Nails into my length-deficient neck. With her opinion made clear, Miss Clapp launched into a lesson on hair-teasing, offering the best ways to make it mountain-high. Big hair was one advantage of the '80s for a short girl. A little Aqua Net, and I was five foot three.

Our participation culminated in the P7 Promenade, a fashion show sponsored by Sears. There we'd flash our Park Seven smiles and parade our Park Seven best in front of hundreds—well, dozens—well . . . some of the parents.

"Ladies, I have wonderful news," Miss Clapp announced. "You're going to strut on the Orange Julius stage." My stomach sank. I had no desire to make a fool of myself before the world—or, at least, anyone at Maryvale Mall that Thursday.

To get ready, we began the process of wardrobe styling—little more than paging through old copies of *Mademoiselle*. On every cover, a chiseled, Nordic girl with a tiny nose and long neck peered at me as if to say, "What the fuck is wrong with you, Lila?" The closest inspiration I found was a Calgon ad. Take me the fuck away.

Shopping with the Park Seven girls was no less traumatic. They gleefully giggled as they pored over the neon fashion in the juniors department. One by one, each emerged from the dressing room, looking runway ready. Meanwhile, the fitting room mirror became a funhouse mirror when I stood before it. Sensing my frustration, an over-coiffed saleswoman pulled me aside and whispered, "Honey, we have a section for people like *you*," and pointed directly to the Kids Konnection sign.

I kicked off my platform heels in humiliation and walked over to Tower Records. Captivated by overflowing racks of vibrant album covers, I nearly leapt ten feet when a gorgeous clerk named Rob interrupted my enthrall. "Got something against shoes?" he asked, glancing at my naked feet. I recognized him from the jazz trio that performed outside Joe's Pub across from Park Seven. Rob played piano like a tall, blue-eyed Herbie Hancock—mysterious, complex, and cool.

Thoroughly embarrassed, I managed to utter, "Uh, where is the jazz section?" to which he quizzically looked up at the Jazz/Big Band sign. Right. Above. My. Head. Mortified, I put on the demo headphones, called up some Dave Brubeck, and transported myself far away. That record store was my juniors department. Everything fit me perfectly.

During our final class, Miss Clapp handed out flyers for the P7 Promenade made on a mimeograph machine older than she was. As she dropped them on the table, the smell of duplicating fluid for once overpowered the acetone and bergamot perfume that saturated the room. Body spray was all the rage at Park Seven. Before class, I'd often walk into the bathroom to find the girls singing the Enjoli jingle that flooded our airwaves: a quasi-feminist ode to bringing home the bacon then serving it to your man—apparently powered by perfume.

While the other Park Seven girls oohed and aahed over Miss Clapp's flyers, I felt sick at the sight of them. "Ladies, share these with your family and friends," she exclaimed. "And as always, make the stage your own." As soon as I left, I tossed my stack into the bin at the Taco Bell, crumpled atop a half-eaten Enchirito.

The days before the P7 Promenade filled me with dread. Every morning, my pounding heart awakened me before my alarm could. Would I stick out like an overweight, under-tall thumb? Would I trip in those heels, leaving my dignity on the Orange Julius stage?

I vowed to put together my runway outfit once and for all. With little time left, I threw open my closet door and grabbed the first thing I saw, a Gloria Vanderbilt denim skirt, the price tag still hanging. Sucking in my breath, I wriggled it on. The waist fit perfectly, but the length looked more suited for Amish Country. It fell far below my knees. Desperately, I grabbed some scissors and chopped off the bottom. Take that, juniors department!

Energized, I riffled through my dresser and pulled out an old Miles Davis T-shirt. I tried on the skirt and top, then threw on my scarlet Nine West heels. "Not bad," I thought, looking in the mirror. But something was missing. Furiously, I scoured my room for the right accessory. A scarf? Too frilly. My treble clef pendant? Too small. As I slammed the drawer closed, the perfect solution beckoned atop the dresser: my Selmer Mark VI soprano sax. I slapped on the neck strap and wore it like a glimmering jazz talisman.

I slept perfectly that night. The next day, I arrived at Maryvale Mall in full regalia and headed to the stage. Much to my relief, I found only a sea of moms—Carols, Barbaras, and the occasional Nancy—sitting in the audience. But as I rounded the corner to join the other girls, my stomach dropped. All the confidence I'd possessed the night before drained out of me. Did I look OK? Would they laugh at my clothes? Would I be mistaken for a runaway pre-teen from Kids Konnection?

Timidly, I approached the girls from behind, trying not to attract their attention. They looked exquisite, adorned in beautiful dresses with sequins and satin and silk. "Maybe it's not too late to run," I thought.

But then it was too late.

"Line up, ladies," Miss Clapp called out. "It's showtime!" She signaled to none other than Rob from Tower Records, sitting by the stage with a Panasonic boombox. As he caught my eye, my cheeks matched my ruby-red heels. The boombox shuddered with *Aaaaah, Freak Out!* and the show began.

When I stepped onto the stage, the spotlight blinded my eyes, a blessing in disguise, really; I couldn't see the audience at all. Nearing the edge of the runway, saxophone hanging from my neck, I was overcome by the pulsating rhythm of the music and the excitement of the crowd. "Make the stage your own!" I thought, bathed in an overwhelming sense of nothing to lose.

And so, with the disco sounds of Le Chic in the background, I grabbed my horn with both hands, mouthpiece to mouth, and let loose with a soulful cadenza in time to the music. I played and played as the crowd roared and my heart sang right along. I felt beautiful—Tiffany-like but in a Lila sort of way.

When the show ended, Miss Clapp gathered us behind the stage. "Ladies, I am so proud," she exclaimed. "You were stunning, each and every one." And I swore she looked right at me.

As I left the show, heels in hand once again, Tower Records Rob caught my eye. "Hey, shoes," he said. "You sounded a bit like Coltrane there! Wanna join us next Monday at Joe's?"

Now that was a Monday worth looking forward to. Music to my ears, no heels required.

When All I Had Was the Setting Sun

Suzi Finkelstein

S ome people have said that my story never happened, that it couldn't have happened. But my ex-husband Norman, an Aruban fisherman named Patrick, and I know the truth.

My life with Norman started as a love affair in law school. We worked during the day; Norman was a sergeant in the NYPD, leading an undercover narcotics unit, and I set up risk management programs in city hospitals. We played Beatles songs in our small apartment or sat on the docks over the East River and devised a plan. Graduate, have a small wedding, move to California, and start a family. We had gone to Aruba to celebrate getting engaged.

Standing on the dock in Aruba, we were excited to go sailing alone. We figured we'd go out for a few hours and then be back in time for a sunset dinner. We kissed as we stepped onto the fifteen-foot sailboat. It was noon, and there was not a cloud in the sky. We pushed away from the dock; I smelled the salt air and felt the warm Caribbean breeze. I pointed out a large seagull as we glided across the mirror-like bay.

After thirty minutes, the winds picked up, and I pushed my hair back from my face. Suddenly, we were surrounded by rough water. I looked out to the horizon. Lightning bolts, then thunder. The wind howled. Large waves crested and approached us. "Norman, it's a storm. We need to turn around now." Just then, a powerful wave crashed over the bow, hitting me in the face. "Norman, we need to go back."

I saw him grip the tiller. "I can't turn the boat around."

I tried to stop the boom from swinging, but a wave crashed over me, and I was plunged into the cold, dark sea. I tried to push myself to the surface, but an unrelenting current kept me down. I kicked my legs and forced my way to the surface. "Norman, help me." I turned in a circle, desperate to see him, then shouted, "Bring the boat closer so I can get on."

I dog-paddled while spinning around, frantically looking for the boat. Was it gone? Had it capsized? Was Norman in the water nearby? I would swim, look for him. But as I lifted my arm, even stronger waves crushed me. The ice-cold water caused my hands and feet to curl. I spiraled down faster, deeper into the black darkness. I told myself, *Push up, you must get back to the surface and look for Norman*. I saw a ray of sunlight, then burst through a wave to get to the surface. Air.

Fear took over every cell in my body. I was alone. What was I going to do? Another wave. Helpless, I gasped for air. I looked up to see the sun through the clouds. There was the answer: *Follow the sun; it will take you back to land*. And then I lost sight of the sun, surrounded by a swarm of dark bubbles. The current had pulled me under a third time. *Which way is up?* My head pounded from the pressure; my chest felt as if it was about to explode. Then I heard a different voice within: *SURRENDER. There is no future. You are alone in the endless sea. Your death is imminent. Let go.*

The water was so cold that my legs went numb, and I fell deeper into the water. What would it feel like when my life forces eased and I could no longer move? I saw Norman's face and remembered making sweet love. Suddenly, I entered a patch of warm water and noticed the current had stopped. A stronger voice inside me said, *This is your chance; get to the surface. You're not going to die, NOT HERE! NOT NOW!* I moved my arms, then felt my legs move. I swam through darkness and broke through to the surface, only to be overcome with a new terror. What was below me? Sharks? A poisonous octopus? Deadly sea snakes?

My heart pounded as I told myself, *Fight for your life, for Norman's life.* Follow the sun; remember the seagulls. I felt a surge of life force, and I swam. Nothing was going to stop me. I hummed "Norwegian Wood" and then "Lucy in the Sky with Diamonds." I stopped and rested, singing "Here Comes the Sun." The sun was lower in the sky, now a crimson red. My legs cramped. My skin felt dry. How long had I been in the water? What would I do when the sky turned black? All the swimming, the hours in the water, had been for naught. Why had I fought a battle I couldn't win? Then, I saw a seagull circling above me. *I must be close to land.*

Suddenly, I heard a man with a thick accent say, "Give me your hand!" Was the bird talking to me? "Hurry, give me your hand before you go under." I reached up, and a strong hand grabbed my arm. "I've got you," he said, then lifted me into a small wooden boat. I shivered. He removed his shirt and wrapped it around my shoulders. "You need to get warm. My village is close." Though his voice was reassuring, my body convulsed, and I vomited. "I saw something flapping in the water," he said. "I thought it was an injured bird."

My teeth chattered. He said, "My name is Patrick, and my family hut is near the shore. My wife will help you." Where had he come from? Had Norman sent him to look for me? He handed me a flask and helped me take a sip. "Hold on. We're almost there." I could see a few huts on the beach. I found my voice. "Wait. We must find my fiancé before it's too late. He may still be alive."

Patrick pulled me close. "I will look for him for a few minutes, but I must get you into the hut to warm up." He turned the boat around and zigzagged across the water, blowing a whistle. Suddenly, Patrick stopped the engine, and we pulled alongside the sailboat. The sail was down. Norman was standing up and tied into the boat. Norman's eyes narrowed. "Where the fuck have you been? Didn't you know I was in trouble out here?"

"Get in. She needs medical help; she's going into shock." Norman climbed into the fishing boat. He looked different to me, no longer a gentle, smiling man. When we reached the beach, Patrick jumped out and pulled the boat onto the sand. He carried me into a small hut and put me on a cot. Patrick's tall, round wife moved toward me, carrying cotton sheets to wrap me in. Patrick brought her a bag of plants. Her voice was calm. "This is fresh aloe; it will help heal your skin." The plant felt cooling on my skin. She spoon-fed me warm coconut soup, and I fell asleep. Norman came in the morning, saying he had gotten a ride back to the resort, and talked about changing our flights. He looked at Patrick. "Can I pay you?"

"No money. I'm glad I could help her; it is a miracle she's alive." Patrick's wife handed me a bag of aloe. "Put this on every two hours; you must drink water, and no sun." She hugged me. "You are very brave." Patrick lifted me and put me in the backseat of the cab. As we drove back to the resort, I heard birds chirping. I had survived. I looked at Norman. "What happened? Why didn't you try to get me back on board?"

"I panicked; I saw you go over and thought I was going over too."

"Why didn't you pull down the sail and try to stop the boat?" No answer. "I was out there in the water for hours. Did you ever think I had drowned?"

"No, I knew you were a strong swimmer, that you would come find me."

What was he saying? Did he not understand the danger? "Why were you tied into the boat?"

Growing impatient, he shouted. "If I went over, I would have drowned. The real question is, why did it take so long to get to me? Didn't you know I was in trouble out there?"

I needed to ask one more question. "Why were you shouting and cursing at me when we found you?" Sweat poured down his face. He looked at his feet, "I was alone out there. I was afraid I was going to die." An hour later, I sat in our room and looked at the clear, calm bay. Why hadn't he listened to my shouts that we needed to go back?

I didn't tell many people what had happened when we returned home. I wondered if he was embarrassed that he froze. Still, we got married, moved to California, and had two children. We lived together for thirty years. Whenever a storm came in, I would think about Patrick telling me, "Take my hand; I've got you." Then I'd think about Norman, tied to the boat, shouting at me. Over the years, this pattern repeated. In the face of an emergency, Norman never showed up. Now that I've left him, I can tell the full story. People ask me why I married him after the boating accident. My answer: "I loved him; I hoped he would change."

Two years ago, Norman called to apologize for what happened in Aruba. I asked him why he never thanked me for saving his life. His answer was, "I'll think about it."

FORGED BY STEEL

K'CEE SCOGGINS

I'm a reader. I'm a reader because the only escape I have from our ramshackle farmhouse comes from the books I swipe from Momma's forgotten stash under the coffee table. I bring home books from the school library, too, but they're not the same as Momma's books. I read late at night beneath my shabby Raggedy Ann and Andy quilt with the help of my yellow flashlight. The books are mostly tattered Harlequin romances with outlines of dog-eared bookmarks Momma left behind on the pages, but the Danielle Steel paperbacks are my favorite. On the back of each book is a glamour portrait of Ms. Steel with the quote, "Everybody reads Danielle Steel." I wish I was like everybody else, but I know I'm not.

Plus, Ms. Steel is beautiful. I love her hair, and her clothes mesmerize me. Some nights, I imagine fading into the picture with Ms. Steel. She looks wise and elegant, like the kind of lady Momma preaches about wanting me to be one day. Momma's beautiful too. She just doesn't know it. She has curly jet-black hair and perfect white teeth that peek out when she smiles. Momma doesn't smile much anymore unless it's when she's pretending our life isn't hell.

At twelve years old, I ain't even pretty, much less beautiful. My hair is damaged from a bad perm, but Momma swears I'm stylish. To hell with pretty and stylish anyway: I'm strong. I bet I can ride a horse better than any kid in Oklahoma. I'll cuss a little, but I've never heard Momma say one bad word.

Momma took down the pictures hanging on the walls today. I understand why she did it. Roger, my stepfather, is due to return home any minute from being out on the road hauling cattle. I call him "Dad" to his face, but that's only because Momma says it makes things easier. I don't know my real father. Roger reminds me my father ran off because Momma was poor, and my father traded us in for a college degree and a paid-off Porsche. Galloping my mare Ruby through the pasture feels like freedom to me. When I grow up, I'm going to buy a white Ford Mustang. I figure driving that Mustang will feel the same way.

I stay outside as much as possible and draw circles with my finger in the red dirt near our vegetable garden's entrance. Momma catches me as she beckons me to come in for dinner; I smell the scent of fried okra and hamburger patties drifting through the air.

"What are you doing, baby?" she asks softly.

"Nothin', Momma. I'm comin'."

The red dirt holds all my dreams and secrets.

Momma and I are a team. Tonight, I help Momma by stirring sugar into a pitcher of freshly brewed tea with a big wooden spoon that's beginning to crack at the end.

"Momma, we need a new spoon," I say, as I hold it up for her to see.

Momma looks over from setting plates and glasses down on the kitchen table. "I'll buy a new one the next time I go to town. That one has seen too much use."

At that moment, I hear the front door slam. I drop the spoon into the sink. Roger's here. Momma forms a tight smile on her face, the one that doesn't show her teeth, and gives me a pleading look: *Be nice, K'Cee. Just be nice.* I don't like letting Momma down, so I straighten my shoulders and nod slightly as I carefully move the tea pitcher from the counter to the table. Roger struts into the kitchen and plops down into the chair at the head of the table.

When Roger enters a room, it feels like being stuck inside a vacuum cleaner bag I can't escape from. The only thing I appreciate about Roger is I can usually smell him before I see him. He stinks like diesel fuel from working on his semitruck. His belly hangs over his Wrangler jeans, and he's too big to wear a belt. Instead, he wears navy-blue suspenders to keep his pants from falling. Sometimes, I daydream about unsnapping one side of his suspenders. I bet he would topple right over and break his thick neck. I figure Jesus disapproves of my daydreams.

Roger coolly asks, "What have you two worthless pieces of shit been doing while I've been gone?"

Momma ain't worthless. I ain't a piece of shit. I repeat the mantra in my head as I sit down across from Momma and directly next to Roger. Momma pours him a glass of tea and hurriedly tells him how we've cleaned the hog pens and the chicken coop today. She also mentions that I got As in math and English. I see Roger's jaw clench.

Dangit, Momma. Why did you mention my grades? Tonight is not the night. I'm a straight-A student; it's a fact that infuriates Roger. I make good grades just to spite him, and I think he knows that. He doesn't say anything as he stabs with a fork the fried okra Momma has placed on his plate.

Momma makes the best fried okra in Oklahoma. She breads it with cornmeal, a pinch of flour, garlic salt, and black pepper. I hate that he's stabbing the okra and looking at Momma like he wants to kill her. *Why can't he just eat it?*

"Can I paint my toenails after dinner?"

Roger picks up his mason jar full of sweet tea and throws it toward the sink. I don't flinch as it shatters on the peeled-up linoleum floor. Momma jumps up to find the broom and dustpan. She's crying a little. Thankfully, he doesn't see her tears. I double down and ask the question again, this time with a mouthful of fried okra. I know I need to keep him distracted.

He explodes out of his chair and shouts, "No! Only whores paint their toenails!"

"Okay, I was only wonderin'," I reply, shrugging my shoulders as I swallow the okra.

Momma and Roger sit back down, and we finish our dinner in silence. *I don't even know what a whore is exactly. If they wear polish on their toes, then they're alright by me.*

The following morning, I woke up to Roger pulling me out of bed by my hair and dragging me outside. My body feels like it's on fire as Roger struggles to pull me through the back screen door.

He's still yanking my hair and demands, "Look at the mess you've made!"

After rubbing my eyes, trying to adjust to the morning sun, I look toward the barn where we keep the hogs. *Where's Momma?* The rusted metal drinking trough has water bubbling out all over the pasture.

"I'm sorry. I was readin', and I forgot to turn the faucet off yesterday."

Roger shouts, "You have an excuse for everything. You always got your head in a damn book!"

He releases my hair. Roger's knuckles are white as he squeezes my right arm. He drags me back inside the house and down the hallway. I don't fight back as we stumble through the hallway together. If I do, he will just make it harder on me. We reach my bedroom.

He throws me onto the bed and asks, "Where's the book?"

I need to think fast. I have two choices: *Sweet Valley High* or the Steel book hidden underneath it. I decide to grab the Steel book off the nightstand, causing my flashlight to fall to the floor. I know he's going to hurt the book, and I am seething. I don't want to explain to the librarian why I didn't return a book. I'm ashamed of my life, and she wouldn't understand. Nobody understands.

Shit, I'm busted. He's going to find out I've been swipin' Momma's books. Still, it's better than telling the truth to the librarian. I stand up, ignore the flashlight, and hand him the book.

Roger doesn't look down to read the title or the author. He furiously begins tearing the pages out one by one.

I hate him. I won't let him see me cry. I smile up at him as the pages flutter across my bedroom carpet.

In response to my smile, before he throws what's left of the book to the floor, he spits snuff on it. He turns and walks out of my room.

God, he's gross.

The front door violently rattles open, and slams shut. I hear Roger's pickup truck fire up outside. Momma quietly enters my bedroom. She smells like Dove soap, and her dark hair is wet. I'm down on my hands and knees, picking up the book pages. Momma bends down and helps me. After we finish, we both sit on my bed. She has a swollen eye; it'll be black tomorrow.

"Momma, did he do that because of me?"

Momma smiles, this time showing me her teeth. "No, baby. God, no." Momma looks down at the pages she's holding; her hands begin to tremble. "You're reading a Danielle Steel book? *Malice*?"

I hold my breath and nod my head. "I've only read a page, Momma. I mainly like lookin' at Ms. Steel's picture."

Momma gathers me up and hugs me tight; I finally allow my tears to fall.

"You listen to me, K'Cee LouAnn. We're going to get the fuck out of here."

It's the first time I've ever heard Momma say a bad word.

Classic Vinyl

Hannah Andrews

My math, which is admittedly sub-par, put Barb at about sixty-eight. My mind painted her as gray-haired, apple-cheeked, grandmotherly. I expected a whisper of a woman—a sort of folksong, maybe smooth jazz. I got nothing of the sort. What I got was pure rock and roll.

"I just knew you'd find us someday. What took you so long?" Barb began. Her voice was syrupy, excited. She sounded more teen than boomer.

What took me so long? Well, it took me forty-nine years to begin my search, then about one year of frantic digging. That month, though, in January 2020, everything sped up like a record, one played at the wrong speed. I confirmed both the identity and death of my biological mother. I stumbled upon the existence of a half brother. A week later, said brother, Justin, phoned me and, upon discovering we lived in the same city, invited me to lunch. The very next day, I saw photos of our shared mother for the first time and broke bread with the first biological relative I'd ever met.

It was surreal—finally seeing faces that looked like me. I should've just taken a beat to compose myself, but as I was leaving, Justin told me that Barb, our mother's longtime bestie, insisted I call. The instant I arrived home, head still spinning, I dialed. She was practically manic. I was in shock. I reduced the volume on my earbuds. She was not a soft-spoken woman.

Barb barreled headlong into a mostly one-sided conversation about everything and nothing, how they spent their lives together, how they loved that movie *Beaches*—did I know it? How she'd discovered my mom's secret one day at Lake Michigan.

"I saw her stomach and was all, 'Eww, what happened to you,' and your mom just starts bawling, tells me she gave away a baby at sixteen. I was so young and dumb I didn't even know what stretch marks were. She had this perfect little figure, but ooh, boy, you left your mark on her."

I sat in stunned silence. *I left my mark. My birth mother never forgot me.*

"Your mom was my best friend in life. My whole life. Well, 'cept that time she got pissed at me, told everyone I was dead. Not just 'dead to her,' full-on dead. Ha!" This was not an actual laugh, but rather the word, belted with great gusto—Ha!

I giggled, relaxed, and let myself become entangled in her web of warmth and wit.

"Your mom was whip-smart and hilarious. Such a brat. I'd leave her notes, and she'd correct 'em with a friggin' red pen. Ha!" Then, more quietly, "I miss her every day. She made me promise to tell Justin about you. 'You tell him he's got a big sister out there somewhere.' I did, at her funeral, not the best idea. It just kinda came out—he thought I was crazy. Did he tell ya?"

"Yeah, he said he thought you, umm, imagined it."

"Ha! Aww, honey, I got so many stories for you."

I felt a catch in my throat—*so many stories.* I'd never had any. Now, this zany woman had "so many" just for me. I clung to every syllable of Barb's manic monologue.

My iPhone buzzed. "That's me sending you pictures. Look at us—so young." Barbara sang.

My phone danced on the table, vibrating with each incoming photo. I scrolled in awe. They were the epitome of '70s and '80s glam. Blond Barb had a fabulous Farrah Fawcett flip. My mother, Candy, had a smile bigger than Carly Simon and a magnificent messy mane of black curls. Flawless faces smushed together in photo after photo. They wore short-shorts and tube tops, slinky dresses, and painted-on jeans with halter tops. Fashion plates and foxy.

Justin, eighteen years my junior, had shared pictures from his mother-son memory book earlier that day. These, though, were wholly different—a slice of time after me but before him. Close to two decades' worth of decadence. Instagram-worthy images long before that was even a thing.

"We met when we were still teens. Backstage. We were both dating guys in that band. Ever hear of—" and then she named my second-favorite band ever.

"Barb, I'm fifty, not twelve. Of course I've heard of them. I love them."

"Us too," she laughed, then brazenly, shamelessly began rattling off an impressive, rather lengthy list of their rock and roll conquests as if she were casually leafing through my teen trove of vinyl, peeling posters off my wall. Barb and Candy had been brought together by music, or rather, the makers of. They remained inseparable the rest of their lives, or at least the rest of Candy's.

"We weren't groupies," Barb clarified. "More like—"

"VIPS?" I asked with a giggle.

"You got it, honey. Exactly!" She laughed.

Wait, I'd met one of those boyfriends. "Hey, I think I met that one dude at a charity rock event in Vegas—'08, maybe?" I grasped at the vodka-coated memory. An aging rock god I'd met after the concert, a friend of my friend, but was he maybe my dad? Was that why I'd taken so easily to the piano, why I was the *Rain Man* of song lyrics and could rattle off any song I'd heard, ever, verbatim? Or maybe my dad was some other rock star? *Shit, was my papa LITERALLY a Rolling Stone?*

"Oh no, kiddo," Barb said. "Your dad was before all the rock stars—some blond college kid. I never knew him, but Candy kept a photo; I have it somewhere. She never said a bad word about him. Remember I said when your mom was mad at someone, she'd just cut 'em out like a—" She stopped. I thought I heard her choke back tears.

She must have tripped over the c *word.* Candy died of liver cancer in 2009 at age fifty-seven. Barb remained silent. I sensed her slowly sinking, sinking. *Don't let her drown—say something.*

"Barb, did Justin tell you I lived right down the street from you all in '03? Isn't that weird?" I'd practically moved next door to them in Venice Beach, just two blocks away. It was as if we were unknowingly tethered. Justin and I had discovered that fact in our first conversation, which I had to remind myself was just the day before. What a strange twenty-four hours it had been.

"Oh, honey, you get it, right?" she cut me off, bobbing to the surface, fully buoyant. "That was the universe trying to reconnect you. You and Candy, just circling each other."

Then I sank, pulled down by the parallel universe of it all, so close, maybe passing each other on the street, moving in stereo. Parallel universes, though, by their very nature, don't intersect. They just pile atop each other like stacked sheets of paper in an unreadable novel.

"She looked for you," Barbara said. "Hired a PI and everything." The sentence floated above me like a cartoon bubble. *Why did I wait so long, too long, to search?*

Barb and I exchanged more photos, our phones filled with lives lived, missed, lost.

"You look like her—same beauty mark and everything, 'cept on the opposite side like a mirror." Barb couldn't have known the weight of that sentence. I'd never looked like anyone, never been a reflection, let alone a mirror image, of anyone. Finally, seeing my biological mother's face, it was almost as if I were seeing myself for the first time.

I plugged in my phone and cranked up the volume. Barb's voice enveloped me like a stadium rock anthem. She was amped up to eleven. I wanted to hold up a lighter and sway. Her stories sang to me—lyrics to a song I'd both never and always known.

"I called your grandma," Barb hissed. "She swears she doesn't remember, but I know she does. She kicked Candy out. That's how your mom ended up at one of those unwed mothers' homes. They fought about it for years, right in front of me. You gotta understand how the world was back then."

"I know, I do."

I didn't. Of course, I knew, just a few years after my birth, things began changing exponentially for women—that the world for my generation was far different from the previous. What I couldn't fathom was any mother throwing her pregnant daughter out on the street, ever. Still, I ached to know my grandmother, my heritage. Maybe Barb could convince her to talk to me. *Please don't let her throw me away again, Barb.*

"She doesn't think you're Candy's baby. I'll work on her. We're close. She's a good woman, just hard-headed," Barb assured me. "She told me to let sleeping dogs lie, but I said nope, I'm talking to Candy's baby." Barb was defiant yet sugary sweet. "Honey, come visit me. I got your mom's ashes still. I live on the beach, but I've never scattered 'em. I think I must have been waiting for you."

My beautiful birth mother was gone forever. My grandmother was alive but aloof. Just up the coast, though, former and forever blond bombshell Barb had been waiting for me. A real-life rock goddess to sing me stories and fill my soundtrack with liner notes. It was the trippiest and most beautiful phone call of my life. Barb was a treasure. She was classic vinyl.

Two hours and a lifetime later, we finally said goodbye.

An instant after that, she texted, "I told Candy I'd look after Justin. Now I got both of Candy's babies."

CRAYON YELLOW SUN

C.A. GILCHRIST

It's early evening, just past dinner. I'm forty-two days into my eighth year on earth. So far, it's not going well, but today, at least, they aren't yelling so much. I'm sitting on the living room floor. A man on the TV in a thin tie is talking about President Nixon as I play with my spacemen. They are fighting off another alien horde, the third this week.

Mom drags a dining room chair into the room. The chair legs make furrows in the thick carpet, like sled tracks in green shag snow. Mom sits and balances my gurgling baby brother on her lap. He is chewing on a yellow plastic ring, spit running down his chubby arms.

Across from them, sitting on the low-slung sofa, is my father, holding his newspaper in both hands. He is still, black-rim glasses low on his nose. Mom starts talking. He focuses on the paper and gives it a quick shuffle as if to say, "*Not now. I'm reading, can't you see?*" He looks up, and it seems that he is seeing the tableau for the first time, but I know better. He is keenly aware of everything and all of us. He always is.

Since the day my baby brother arrived, my mother's new-baby shine has faded like an old photograph. Her smiles for him are still present, but they increasingly look hollow and vanish when he looks away from her face. Dad and I noticed and pretended it would be okay—until pretending was no longer possible.

She draws a large breath. "Al, I need to tell you something. Al, I have rabies. I know it's rabies because of the dripping in my head. Al, you and the boys have it too. I've been smelling those awful smells again. It's the demons. These are warnings from God that he will destroy the world any second. We aren't ready, Al; we really aren't ready. I'm afraid for the boys."

For a second, my father's mask of bravado slips. My father sees it now. He really sees it. It's not what he thought it was. There have been other signs, but a corner has been turned. Every inch of his body is tense, like the leg of a lion I saw at the zoo just before it pounced. The newspaper in his hands is forgotten, frozen, like it's been transmuted into sheet metal by an invisible alchemist. I feel Dad take each of his words out and weigh them carefully.

He speaks, his voice containing a tension he hopes will go unnoticed. "I'm sure they are both okay, hun. How about I hold him and take a look."

Like him, I am sensitive and sense the fear between the words. Almost, Dad, almost.

He reaches out to take my brother. The newspaper drops and returns to its natural molecular state. It ruffles to the ground. I see a partial headline, "*Dead in Overnight—*" before it flattens.

My mother pulls my baby brother in tighter to her chest. She looks at me, my father, and back to my brother, shaking her head. "No, Al. It's no use. We are dying."

"Please. Give. Him. To. Me."

"But—"

"Now. Please."

Tears flow from her eyes, dragging matching mascara lines down her cheeks. She wordlessly hands my brother over, gets up, and goes to the bedroom. The door shuts behind her with a soft click.

My father rises. He slides the baby into my hands. "Hold your brother," he says.

My father goes to the kitchen and makes a call. His hand is cupped over the receiver as he talks. He nods as he listens, his hand fiddling with the magnets on the refrigerator. My crayon drawing of four green stick figures standing in front of our blue house under a yellow sun escapes its last magnet and falls to the floor. Dad leaves it there. He hangs up the phone as if the receiver is made of glass and, if he's not careful, it will shatter into a million shards. He is at the bedroom door, opening it just enough to let him pass through, but no more. The house is quiet. It, too, is waiting, tensing, tightening.

A "caa" from my brother breaks the silence. His little fingers have found their way to my mouth. He grabs my lower lip. His nails are sharp, but I don't react. I will him to be quiet so I can hear what's happening. The pain in my chest reminds me to breathe. I take a breath. I hold it.

"Caabluur," my brother coos.

"Shhh," I whisper.

Like a Bernini sculpture, we are locked, waiting. My brother's cheek is pressed against mine, and I smell his strawberry-milk breath. A knock at the front door cracks our pose. My father comes out of the bedroom and closes the door quickly behind him. He opens the front door to admit the minister.

I can't hear the entire conversation, but some words punch through like cotton-wrapped bullets. " . . . sick . . . hurt . . . demons . . . danger . . . self . . . hospital . . . help . . . baby . . ."

The minister follows my father into the bedroom. An eternity passes. They come out. There is a quorum. I sense a decision has been made. My father takes a knee before us.

He takes my baby brother from my arms. "Everything is okay."

"No, it isn't," I say.

He looks me in the eyes. His eyes are gray—gray like valiant steel. He wipes my tears away with his thumb, a thumb calloused from hard work.

"Everything will be okay."

He draws me in with his free arm, squeezes me tight, and lifts me to a safer height. Over his shoulder, I see through the open bedroom door the side silhouette of my mother sitting on the edge of the bed, her arms resting on her knees. Palms up, head down. There is a tissue in her left hand. She drops it. Time slows, and it falls like the forgotten feather of a mourning dove. A single needle of ice, thinner than an eyelash, penetrates my heart as the tissue hits the ground.

No, everything will not be okay.

A siren far off. Then closer, louder. A dog barks twice. The siren comes even closer. Two dogs bark. The siren is here. Right here. Now. Red light sprays against the front curtains. Harder knocks on the door. Two men come in.

The minister takes my brother. He leads me to my bedroom. He says he will sit with us while my father leaves for a bit. I don't speak. I lay down. The sirens and lights leave. Sleep takes me.

I awake, and my father's mother stands over me with my brother in her arms. She mumbles something and leaves for the kitchen. Nana Mumbles is my nickname for her. She barely speaks and never directly to me. I don't think she likes me much.

"Where's Dad?"

"Bcks oon."

"Back soon?" I ask. She nods.

She makes me a bowl of Cheerios and drops it in front of me. I worry that the drops of milk will leave marks on the table, so I clean them up. I think about asking more questions, but I don't. I finish my Cheerios and go to my room. I want to read, but I can't. Instead, I pray. I pray that my mother and little brother will be okay. I pray that my father will be okay and that they will come home soon. The sound of my father arriving interrupts my prayers. I run out to him and into his arms.

"Where's Mom?"

"Your mom . . ." He stops and starts again. "Your mom has been feeling sick for a while. The doctor thought it might be best if she stayed at the hospital for a few days."

"Why? How many days? Can we see her?"

"Sometimes moms get tired from all the hard work they do and need a rest. Grandma will be taking care of you when I can't. While I am at work, I need you to be the man of the house."

Being called a man feels good, and I assure him I'm ready for the task. I feel taller.

A few days without Mom turns into three, then five, then more. I see the wear it is taking on my father. His movements are overly precise, and his jaw is always clenched. I repeatedly ask him when she will be home. He says "soon" and nothing more.

⚜

Fifty-one days into my eighth year on earth, I am sitting on the living room floor, drawing with my crayons. Without warning, my mother comes in the front door, her coat billowing behind her like a superhero's cape. My father follows her in, holding a small suitcase. She takes my brother from my grandmother, and he lights up like a firefly. She kisses me on the head as she walks past to sit on the sofa, her hand trailing a band of warmth across my shoulders. I want to hug her, but I don't know if it's allowed.

"I'm glad you're home. Why were you gone for so long?" I ask.

"That place is awful. The doctors wouldn't let me go. The screams all night kept me—"

My father's hand on her leg stops her. "The important part is that Mom is home," he says.

My mother nods yes and smiles.

My father's jaw relaxes, but his eyes do not.

I hand my mother the drawing. "Are you better now?" I ask.

She looks down at my drawing. The four stick figures look back at her from in front of the blue house.

A single tear falls from her eye onto the yellow sun.

Tower, We're Going Down

Chuck Dunning

September 25, 1978

I sat in the sales meeting at KSDO Radio, staring blankly at the wall. My girlfriend of nearly a year had just gone back to her ex. Life, as I knew it, was over. My stomach was in knots, and I was nursing a slight hangover. The night before, I had driven to the backcountry and sat in my car, drinking Coors and listening to Bonnie Tyler sing "It's a Heartache." As Larry, the sales director, droned on, I felt my eyes wanting to close. I glanced up at the wall clock as it ticked past 9 a.m. Then I heard a loud BOOM outside.

The nine of us turned around and pulled back the curtains. All I saw were the neat homes and manicured yards of the neighborhood below. As I turned back around, assuming it was a sonic boom, the expressions of those facing the windows went white. I looked back to see that a jet plane was now going down. Eyes bulged, mouths gasped, hands flew to lips. Someone cried out, "OH MY GOD. A PASSENGER JET IS CRASHING!"

The ground and windows shook again, and I saw a rising column of thick black smoke spreading huge orange and red flames. The jet hit the ground blocks away, yet close enough to make the building shake. Fire trucks raced toward it.

I couldn't speak, swallow, or look away. As I watched the spectacle of flame and smoke rise into the sky, it struck me like a hammer. I'd just watched a planeload of people die before my eyes. Witnesses on the ground later reported they heard screams coming from the plane and could see faces plastered to the windows as it hurtled to earth. Time froze until Larry yelled, "Chuck! Get downstairs to the newsroom and make sure they see what's just happened!"

I bolted down the stairs to the third floor. At the newsroom door, the news director, who was as big as a linebacker, shoved past me. I entered as folks rushed to the windows. I burst into the on-air booth where the sports director was cheerfully wrapping up his morning program. Without a word, I pulled back the curtains so he could see what was now an inferno.

"Holy shit! What happened?" he stammered.

"PSA jet just crashed not far from here," I blurted.

One of the producers poked her head into the newsroom and said, "Get reporters to the airport, crash site, and PSA headquarters, also to the police and fire command centers, and get the traffic reporter back in the air." I stood hypnotized at the window. I'm not sure I was even breathing. Phones rang around me. Another producer yelled, "I just got a call. A small plane has also crashed at the intersection of 32nd and Polk." I felt an itching in my feet. Anxiety clutched my chest. I wanted to do something.

"What is going on? Where the hell are all the reporters?" the sports director cried out, looking around the room. A producer answered, "They've all been sent out." Jolted from my daze, I called out, "I can go down there. I have a police press pass." Realizing he had no other options, he threw me a tape recorder and microphone, barking, "Get over there, find some people that might have seen the crash. Get them on tape, then get your ass back here."

I took off, covering the two blocks on a dead run, operating on pure adrenaline. I was nearly out of breath and sweat-soaked in the ninety-degree weather when I reached the corner. A small crowd of people were tentatively walking around the wreckage. The main body of the four-passenger Cessna sat in the middle of the street, with the engine and propeller down the block. It hit nose first and flipped on its back, burying part of the cockpit into the pavement.

Then I noticed a pair of legs protruding from under the wreckage, bent at grotesque angles like a ragdoll's, the shoes still on. I stopped short, my stomach in my throat. The only dead person I'd ever seen was my grandfather, neatly dressed and sleeping peacefully in his casket. I looked around my feet, and my stomach roiled when I noticed small chunks of flesh and bits of bone scattered about. I couldn't bear to look into the cockpit, sickened at what else I might see. The police arrived and cordoned the site off.

I entered the crowd. There was no shortage of witnesses, and I captured their reactions as best I could. A woman sobbed, "It was awful. I first saw a flash of light in the sky, heard an explosion, and then saw the two planes coming down. The little one was turning slowly, this guy's legs just hanging there. It was sickening."

With tape in hand, I ran back into the newsroom and handed it to an editor. The newsroom was crackling with nervous energy. I couldn't get the image of the crumpled Cessna and mangled legs out of my brain. A gnawing pit of helplessness sat in my stomach.

Thirty minutes later, Larry pulled me aside. His normally twinkling eyes were dull, his mouth chewing on an unlit pipe. He said in a shaky voice, "A friend of mine just called. The wife of an employee and her three-year-old son were in the vicinity of the crash this morning, and no one's heard from them. Can you get down there and nose around?"

"Sure," I said, wondering if I could locate them and deliver a small nugget of good news. I ran to the command center in the parking lot of St. Augustine High School, about a mile from the crash site, walking past the open doors of the school gymnasium, now serving as a morgue. I paused as I took in the sight: covered bodies on stretchers laid out in neat rows. Two paramedics arrived carrying another sheet-draped stretcher. The fires were out, but smoke was still wafting by with overpowering smells of jet fuel, molten metal, and burning wood. Sweaty, soot-covered police and firefighters scurried back and forth with the haunted look of soldiers returning from battle. I was in the middle of hell.

A firefighter pointed me to a hastily constructed canopy with a Red Cross symbol, a card table, and a sole attendant with a clipboard and walkie-talkie. I handed her the two names. "I'm looking for these two, a three-year-old boy and his mom. We think they were at their babysitter's around the time of the crash."

She looked at a list of names on her clipboard. "Let's see. Nine people have been taken to hospital." My hopes rose. Moments later, she looked up, sadness in her eyes. "I don't see them on this list."

"Is that everyone?"

She looked close to tears. "I'm so sorry."

As I slowly returned to the office, I thought of those soldiers who had to deliver news of a comrade's death to the family. I thought of Larry having to give this news to his friend. As I told him, he slumped in his desk chair and looked at the floor, aimlessly cleaning his pipe. "Okay. I'll let them know."

Hours later, we would find out that mother and son, along with five others, had died on the ground. Searchers found the mangled remnants of her license plate in front of the house where the PSA jet hit. Leaving the newsroom, I saw the headline of the *Evening Tribune*: "AIR TRAGEDY. WORST U.S. AIR CRASH KILLS 144 HERE."

I returned to my office for the first time at about 7 p.m. I leaned my head back and sank into my chair. I thought back on what I had considered so crushing just the night before, when I drank beer in my car and listened to sad songs. I thought back on the boredom and annoyance I felt as the morning meeting droned on. I took a breath and thought of the 137 people innocently boarding those planes this morning: one hundred thirty-five on the PSA flight, two in the Cessna. Perhaps one of them was sad about a breakup, like me. Then, in an instant, in a flash, it was all over.

NEANDERTHAL WOMAN

SARAH CHURCH VOSBURGH

"I want to be in the delivery room when the baby is born."

My mother and I were out for Sunday brunch in the seventh month of my first pregnancy. She was dressed for the occasion—dress, heels, and hair coiffed by an eggbeater. I dwarfed my mother on any day, but today, I was pregnant, feeling large and looming.

She hadn't asked, "Would you like me to be?" or "Can I be helpful?" She'd had a baby once. In the fifties. From a state of unconsciousness. She'd been full of "helpful little tips" all along. For seven months, I had just said, "Oh, thank you," and moved on, careful not to roll my eyes. She didn't stop. "Your grandmother was there to greet you when you were born. She was the first to hold you. It's a family *tradition.*"

"We will make sure you are there too." I acquiesced. How could I leave my lonesome widowed mother out of this? We were all she had left.

"We? Too? What? *He's* not going to be there, is he? He'll never think of you the same if he sees *that.*" She sipped her coffee, scary side-eye over the cup rim. "Besides, you won't hold her right away; you'll be knocked out. I'll take care of her while you come to and make yourself presentable."

Granddam had been a delivery-room nurse at a time when women were "put out" during labor. While I was confident the delivery-room staff were accustomed to take-charge grandparents, they'd not met my mother.

"Mom, he's going to be there because he's the dad, and my husband and birth coach. They are not going to put me out."

"Birth coach? How ridiculous. You need to take advantage of modern medicine." She continued, barely coming up for air. "There is no reason to be so barbaric and endure all that pain."

In the autumn of 1957, having what she thought was false labor, as her C-section was scheduled for ten days later, she had been rolled into the delivery room straight from church at my dad's insistence—coiffed, in her Sunday best, stilettos, and gloves. She was given full-on put-you-out anesthesia and woke up shaved, stitched, clean, and fresh, with a new baby in the nursery. When she was released from the hospital, she dropped me off at Granddam's for a few hours, likewise accessorized, having set her hair the night before, in a shirtwaist dress with the belt on its tightest notch (or so I was oft told), so she could "present well" to go check sales at Lord and Taylor. "Mom, it's how most babies are born these days. It's considered healthy for baby and mom."

"*Who* is this *doctor* you have? You should ask him about putting you out. Then you don't have to be embarrassed when they shave you, and you won't feel it when they sew you back up." I didn't want to argue about shaved nether regions with my mother, now or in labor. Or *ever*.

"Mom, I'm going on the advice of my doctor. *Amy.* I would love to have you there, but you'll need to be supportive." By now, my chest was hard, tight, my breathing shallow. I could feel the fight coming.

"Of course; you have a *woman* doctor. *That's* what this is all about."

Are you fucking kidding me? I wanted to say, but she was my mom. I tried to be gentle.

"Mom, after making her and carrying her and birthing her, it is her father and I who will hold her first. We will happily hand her over to you after I nurse her."

"Wait! Nurse her? You're doing that too?" She was spitting out her words now. "This woman doctor is making you one of those militants. They can give you pills to dry you up. You don't want to get saggy breasts! It's so primitive."

I paused, focusing on the tinkling and hum of the café, using it as a kind of soothing tune to calm my breathing. "Mom, if you would like to be in the delivery room, I'm happy to make it happen. Would you like us to call you when we leave for the hospital or when delivery is closer?"

"What do you mean closer?"

"It's my first, and it may take a while for things to move along. We can play Monopoly." This was her favorite; she was cutthroat—grabbing hotels with glee and a twinkle in her eye.

"I don't want to be waiting around all day being *frivolous;* I'm *busy.* They can give you medicine, so it's quick. Why are you insisting on being so crass, so philistine?!"

I tried for slower, deeper breaths. "We'll call you when it's imminent, Ma." Her next words, all quickly pressed, carried panic behind her annoyance.

"Never *mind,* I don't want to be there for all this ridiculousness. You haven't listened to anything I've told you. You'll never get your body back. No one knew *I* was pregnant until I was eight months, because I wore a girdle."

A bite of over-easy egg in mid-swallow threatened to stick. Her eyes were now full front, no cup rim, bulging. Silence. Swallow. I sipped tea and attempted another nibble of dry toast. She wasn't finished.

"You're already so big, you'll never have a flat stomach again, you won't look good in clothes, and your vagina will be loose. Do it the way I did. When they sew you up, it'll be tighter than a virgin." Wound up and almost yelling, she lamented, "Why won't you take advantage of modern medicine? We live in the twentieth century. You should *not* be having a baby like a Neanderthal woman!"

I never finished breakfast. She noted, "It's a little late in the game to attend to your eating. Better late than never, I guess."

From then on, I avoided anticipatory birth comments when near her. I called her several weeks later to confirm the plan. "Mom, it doesn't sound like you want to be in the delivery room, under the circumstances."

"Well, of course not! How can I condone all this foolishness and irresponsibility? You are taking terrible risks with my granddaughter and with your marriage. Never mind *me*. You've always done your own thing. I don't know why I would expect this to be any different. I'll see her after when, hopefully, you'll approach your parenting in a more reasonable fashion."

"Of course, Mom." *Like just the way you did it?*

Two months hence, we called my mother when leaving for the hospital. With each subsequent update, she expressed displeasure at how long things were taking. When I called with the last update—between close contractions—to let her know her grandgirl's arrival was imminent, her breathless response was simple: "I'm so busy; I'll get there as soon as I can."

After four days of labor, when a plunger finally extracted a stubbornly reluctant neonate, my girl was delivered onto my belly. Our new babe was wiped, swaddled by nurses, and placed in my arms. The complications just minutes ago seemed a distant past.

My husband lay on the bed next to me, her nestled safely between. We were dressed in old T-shirts and sweats. I was comfortable, content, even with a messy, sweaty ponytail and loose vagina. Milk-drunk, cozy, and probably overstimulated, our babe cared not. We had greeted her and said her name. We had told her the story that went with it, and recited poetry as when she was inside, and settled right quick into a three-way cuddle.

My mother made it to the hospital just a couple of hours after birth, flowers in hand, in a reverent hush. She was in awe of her granddaughter, instantly smitten, shedding a tear or two. I handed her our sleeping babe, whom she held alternately close and at a distance, gazing at her face, depositing whispers of kisses on her crown, counting her fingers and toes, exclaiming over and over in her ear, "I wish your grandfather were here." She rocked and sang as she had done for me so many years ago. We took pictures. The world melted away.

Days later, she began anew.

"If you nurse her too often, she'll get fat."

"Why don't you use disposable diapers? I wish I had those when you were a baby."

"You're holding her too much. You're teaching her how to get your attention; it will spoil her."

We were thrilled with the photos we took that arrived in our mailbox the following week when the details had begun to fade. They evoked the sounds, smells, and serenity of those first hours. We studied them lovingly and with awe. Then, "Honey, go back," I said to him. "Is that what I think it is?" There it was: my mother's familiar waist-front fanny pack. Barely concealed was a 9-mm semiautomatic handgun. My mother, serene as could be, in my maternity room with my hours-old daughter in her arms. *Militant, Mom?* I don't know if it was a passive-aggressive move on her part or just habit. I lean toward the former.

A Test of Physics

Amy Lisewski

"*D*ear *Amy, You don't know who I am, but I know you. Eighteen years ago, I made a big mistake.*"

The thick, bright-pink envelope crash-lands on the family dining table inches behind my stack of well-organized high school notebooks. The four-page letter has unfolded from its fleshy pink envelope, waving to me in the June breeze coming in the front door.

It had begun as an ordinary morning for any overconfident high school senior rushing toward adulthood. I just needed to ace today's AP physics exam, graduate next week, and finally, get on with the life I've been dreaming of. I knew this material inside and out, but I was dutifully re-reviewing the laws of physics—*an object in motion will stay in motion unless acted upon by an opposite force*—when my mom came in from the mailbox, sorted through the grocery store fliers, record-club subscriptions, and utility bills, and then dropped the pink envelope on the table.

"Who's it from?"

"There's no return address."

"Maybe a summer camp friend?" Both of us had said one or more of these everyday phrases without interrupting the flow of our lives.

It's 1988, and letters are common. Pen pals are still a thing, although I am not one to keep up with correspondence. But the fact that there is no return address, it's bright pink, and it's late June, a whole month past my May birthday, grabs my attention, and I tear into the envelope.

The first thing I notice is the cursive of someone older than me. Not a camp friend. The lines are too perfect. The "Dear Amy" is too careful.

"You don't know who I am, but I know you. Eighteen years ago . . ." I flip to the last page, where the final word I see is "Cheryl." My birth mother.

With both hands, I push the letter away from my chest, expecting it to soar like a basketball, but it quivers to the table like a demonstration of gravity.

⚜

Being adopted was never a secret for our happy family of five—nine if you count the dogs and hamsters, which I naturally did. Before my two brothers and I could even ask about the birds and the bees, we knew where *we* babies came from. Heck, when I was four, we all piled into Dad's white wood-paneled station wagon and drove to pick up my baby brother from the nuns. "We chose you," our parents said to us, and it was a simplistic yet perfect explanation.

I was born on Mother's Day—the most ironic of days when you're adopted. But my life wasn't an after-school special with the main character searching for "that missing piece of themselves." In my world, your parents were the ones who chose you. And raised you.

I did wonder about my birth mother now and then, but only in fleeting fantasies—a persistent, sneaking feeling that my birth mother was a famous Hollywood actor who just needed to focus on her career. All adoptees have their imaginary stories just like other kids have imaginary friends. I told myself I must have gotten my acting skills from whoever gave birth to me. I wondered which talented actor she was. If only she could make me famous like her! Even if I did figure out who she was, she wouldn't become my real mom. I had one of those already. Her name was Peggy.

⚜

Mistake? This letter is the mistake. This morning is the mistake. Your timing is the mistake. I am an object in motion: forward, confident, happy motion. I do not want to be acted upon by a greater force in the opposite direction. My birth mother's letter slams into my heart and disorients my brain. *No, I don't know you. And I have already decided who you will be.*

I extend my arms tightly and grip the curved edges of the table, creating distance, holding her words back. Panic drives my nails into the layers of Lemon Pledge on my mom's early American oak dining table. I freeze in place.

Looking around, I quickly assess if I have an audience for my unplanned performance. Of course I do. My mother is making my little brother's breakfast in the kitchen, which is right over the dining room's shoulder. She's watched every bit of this scene so far. And my dumb face has just given away that this was no ordinary letter.

I want to flee, but there is no easy way out. Mom is blocking my route. I have to get through her to the driveway where my little green VW Rabbit, my getaway car, is parked. I snap my face back to "everything is fine" mode, but before I can pry my hands free from the table, Mom makes the interception, snapping up the offending words and their stupid bright-pink envelope.

Cut to curiosity. Recognition. Shock. It's like she already knew what it was—knew there'd be an intrusion. Cut to a close-up of tears as she flees down the hallway and slams the door to her bedroom. I hear her dial the yellow rotary phone by her bed. I hear her muffled cries to my father, who's already at work. I faintly hear her voice with shock and panic say, "But, it seems real."

The exit route through the kitchen is now clear. *Shit. Shit. Shit.* I can stay and get that letter back and read the parts between "big mistake" and "Love, Cheryl," or take five quick steps across the kitchen linoleum and go to my exam before she hangs up the phone.

As I rush through the kitchen, I place my unfinished cereal bowl in the sink and wonder, how can two objects, two people, and two completely different realities interact and not cause one to spin off in an unintended direction? What if there are three objects? Two mothers and one daughter. Physics can't explain getting a letter out of the blue when you are eighteen, from a woman claiming to have given birth to you.

⚘

I think of the letter often; it's more present in my mind than my birth mother herself. It took me years to find grace for my teenage self—and for her. I can only imagine how difficult it was to write that letter.

But I chose the exit route and took the physics exam. I got a 95. I didn't ask about the letter, but I know my mom placed it in the bottom drawer of her dresser.

I never read the rest of the letter I never asked to receive.

STUCK

DIANE L. SCHNEIDER, MD

August 1984
Grady Memorial Hospital, Atlanta, Georgia

I saw red. I watched, frozen in horror, as droplets of blood, *my blood,* streamed down my right index finger. Everything proceeded in slow motion, except my heart pounded like I just ran a wind sprint. The med student had made a quick jab with the syringe needle, which was missing the red rubber top, and the tip plunged into my finger.

Oh Lord, please tell me this didn't just happen! Damn, clumsy med student! I scowled at him, and he stared back. I rushed to the sink to wash my hands and squeezed the end of my finger as hard as I could to force more bleeding. I waited impatiently for hot water as I kept my finger under the water flow. I stood there and washed my hands with soap over and over again like someone with an obsessive-compulsive disorder. My chest tightened, and I became lightheaded. I realized I'd started hyperventilating.

Get hold of yourself.
Take deep breaths.
Slow down.

Only seven weeks into my medical internship, and I'm a dead person. The needle inoculated me with blood from a patient who most likely had AIDS. So far, no one has survived having AIDS. It was a death sentence.

I left the room. The med student followed me out. I wanted to inhabit Edvard Munch's famous canvas and let out a primal scream. Instead, I forced out between clenched teeth, "Just get the specimens down to the lab right *now.*" He took the order and made a fast escape.

I immediately dialed the on-call Infectious Diseases fellow, petrified of the consequences. My hands and voice shook. "You know Raymond Rodriquez?"

"Yeah, what's the emergency?" he said, with a sleepy voice.

"It's not him, it's ME." I tried hard to hold myself together. My heart and breathing hadn't calmed down.

"What happened?"

"A needlestick from my bumbling med student."

"Oh, no!" A long pause followed. "Okay, okay. First, scrub your hands with bleach. In the morning, you'll need to report the needlestick to Employee Health."

My mind flashed back to the chief resident's conference at the beginning of August, when our chief had announced a major breakthrough in AIDS. The CDC had proved that exposure to infected blood could cause AIDS in laboratory animals. Chimpanzees developed early symptoms of AIDS after they were infected with the virus by blood inoculation or by giving them plasma from AIDS patients. Our chief had admonished us to be careful. If this virus acted like hepatitis B—a quarter of persons with needlesticks developed infection—then handling blood could be hazardous.

"What about the chimps getting AIDS?" I said, as my voice dropped to a whisper, "Isn't that what just happened to me?"

The fellow tried to calm me down. "Well, there are no reports of transmission by needlesticks in healthcare personnel."

Shit, it would be just my luck to be the first case. I always wanted to make a contribution to medicine. Well, this wasn't the way I envisioned it—the first healthcare worker infected with AIDS.

Guttural queasiness hit me as I riffled through the housekeeper's closet for bleach. The array of chemical-cleaner odors didn't help. I scrubbed my hands with full-strength bleach until they turned chalky white.

My mind raced in sheer panic. I couldn't calm down. My heart thumped rapidly and hard. I needed to talk to my resident, Wayne, who oversaw my work. I woke him up. I talked so fast that all my words ran together.

"AneedlestickwithraymondsbloodjusthappenedIcalledIDscrubbedwithbleach."

"Okay, okay. Slow down. Could you say that again?"

I took several long breaths. I stared down at my stuck finger.

"Are you there?" Wayne asked.

"Yes," I said, and retold the story that vividly replayed once again, to my horror.

"Settle down. The sky is not falling yet."

"Yet. Right. Yet!" I said, with a louder voice. "But how soon will it?"

"Hm-mm," Wayne hesitated.

"What about the chimps?" I screeched, as my jaw tightened. "I just got inoculated like them."

"Hang on, hang on. You know they are working on a blood test to detect the virus."

"Yeah. It will only give me a doomsday warning."

"Let's do some more research."

"You bet I will." I first planned to look up the complete CDC report on the chimp research. I beat myself up because I'd catnapped when the lights dimmed for our chief's presentation. Now the details were important, very important. "The only thing I'm thinking about is death."

"Try to focus on finishing up your work."

I returned to our team's office lightheaded and wobbly. I sat at the table and stared out the window into the night darkness instead of writing on the history and physical forms spread in front of me. Shit. Shit. SHIT! I felt trapped in a surreal *Twilight Zone* episode. I could already hear, "Our dearly departed, Diane."

A few hours later, I sat in morning report, physically present but not mentally. After a thankfully uneventful hour of presentations, I went directly to Employee Health. There, I filled out incident forms about the needlestick. An infection-control nurse reviewed them and interviewed me, then drew blood for testing. "Right now, it's our protocol to ship one sample to the CDC for future testing once there's a specific test for the AIDS virus. So, we'll also need a red-top tube from your patient. This requires consent from both you and your patient."

She filled out the consent, turned it toward me on the desk, and held out a pen. *AIDS* jumped off the page from the diagnosis box next to the patient's name, *Raymond Rodriquez*.

I took a deep breath and pointed to the reason for the blood storage there in black ink: *AIDS*. "We haven't even told him that."

"Well, that might be helpful," she said in a snippy tone. "He'll see it on the form he signs."

We still hadn't told him nor written in his medical record the overarching diagnosis of AIDS. No one wanted to make a mistake, since there was no definitive way to diagnose AIDS. None of us had experience with AIDS. Last year, in the entire state of Georgia, only two dozen patients met the criteria for the diagnosis of AIDS, so we were learning along the way. On top of that, the medical staff at Grady wanted to be as certain as possible before labeling anyone with AIDS, because of the social stigma and fear attached to it. The barrage of news with scary headlines about the growing numbers of AIDS cases and research findings created panic in the public. It fueled a widespread fear of the "gay plague"—or, for that matter, of anyone gay.

Medical professionals, as well as the general public, had many unanswered questions. Could the germs leap to other people even many feet away, or linger on hard surfaces for hours, like a cold virus? Could a mosquito bite transmit the virus, like malaria? Did it take an intimate exchange of body fluids or just a casual exposure for transmission?

I felt for Raymond Rodriquez. A bright spark of life, diminished by this assault on his immune system. He was my first patient with this terrible disease that attacked and killed young, healthy gay men in the prime of their lives. His case heralded the beginning of what was to become a horrible epidemic. The outlook for a cure for this deadly virus didn't appear promising—or even possible. We had no cures for any other viruses, not even the common cold.

So many questions flooded my mind. How long did he have left? Could we at least get him home? What else could we do to provide comfort? But I also couldn't stop the selfish thoughts—*What's going to happen to me?* The events of the past twenty-four hours constituted the absolute worst day of my internship. I felt as if I lived in a modern-day redux of Albert Camus's *The Plague,* which I'd read in Freshman English. The plague transported to 1984 as AIDS, the incurable, indiscriminate disease that felled loved ones.

One moment could change the trajectory of my life. Would a doctor, one day soon, sit at my bedside and deliver terrible news? In April, the HHS secretary set the goal of a vaccine and blood test within two years. I held a glimmer of hope for the promise of a cure, a treatment, a vaccine. But it was already too late for Raymond Rodriquez and others with AIDS to engage in this magical thinking.

GOING ON THE LAM

INDRA GARDINER BOWERS

M aybe I got too comfortable.

It was the summer of 1984, and I had landed my own sweet little apartment less than ten minutes from campus. I paid $100 a month, along with some babysitting for Ginny and Rich, the couple who owned the apartment and the house it was connected to. Rich was a grad student, while Ginny owned a knitting shop in Amherst.

Having filed for his first patent and about to get his doctorate, Rich was being vetted by the federal government for a job at Lawrence Livermore Labs in California. Ginny was whip-smart and funny, and their one-year-old baby Blair endlessly entertained us. I loved living with them—it felt normal, and I hadn't experienced much normal in my life up until then.

With one final semester to go, Julian and I had been dating for over a year. My friends thought he was an odd choice—a bit conservative, a smoker, and career-driven. But we connected intellectually and sexually, and I felt safe with him after years of picking guys who hadn't been emotionally available to me.

Best of all, for the last three years, my mother, father, and stepmother had all been living within a two-hour drive of Amherst, the first time we had all been that close geographically since I was twelve.

After an unhappy marriage that had included many years of prison time, drugs, and massive amounts of resentment, my parents split for good when I was eleven. At thirteen, I moved from NYC to Chapel Hill, North Carolina, with my dad and his now wife, Shreya, while my mom moved to upstate New York to be with her new boyfriend. Over the next eight years, my mother rotated between New York, Jamaica, and India. Years that consisted of letters, occasional phone calls, and a depressing sense of disconnection and abandonment. And then came the miraculous last three years. Dad, Shreya, and our dog Blossom were a functioning, stable family. It was something solid—something I could rely on.

Julian and I had been hanging out in the kitchen that late summer afternoon, doing homework while Rich made dinner. Rich had put an enormous pot on the stove that morning, showing me how he made his mother's gravy, as he called it, with lots of sausage and cans and cans of tomatoes. The house smelled like my favorite red-sauce Italian joint.

Suddenly, the phone rang. It was my father, and he sounded tense.

"Uh, hey Indra, how are you?"

"I'm good. Is everything OK?"

"Well, Shreya and I are just leaving the house on our way to you," he replied. "We need to let you know what's going on."

My stomach sank. I could barely speak. "What's going on?"

"We'll see you soon and tell you when we see you. Gotta go." And he hung up.

My life, at that very moment, was something I had craved and now cherished. But that phone call told me it was all about to end.

As we sat around the dinner table, I felt like I was sitting on a balloon about to pop. Loudly. The problem was no one else knew the balloon was there. As close as we were, no one knew my family's history. My well-schooled ability to hide the truth meant dinner felt like any other night to them. But I knew a storm was coming.

We heard the crunch of wheels in the gravel driveway next to the kitchen as we finished dinner.

After my dad and stepmom stepped out of the car, they opened the back door, and our family dog, Blossom, hopped out. *Um, why is Blossom with them? They usually leave her at home.* My heart raced. My dad's face looked drawn, and Shreya had clearly been crying.

"We need to tell you something," my dad said, looking around at the table full of faces he didn't know all that well. He was not a trusting man; seven years in prison would do that to a person.

"Someone's dropped a dime on me, and we must go. We've packed up the house and are heading west in a couple of days."

Silence.

We all sat there processing what he had just said. Julian, Rich, and Ginny looked at me with quizzical faces. Dropped a dime? *No, this is not a normal dinner conversation.*

"You're leaving?" I slowly asked.

"We have to go on the lam. Now. We're leaving, and you won't be able to reach us," he said. "That's why I think your friends here should know. The police could show up looking for us, and you all need to know what to do."

I was used to the high-stakes world of my family, but my friends had just been thrust into my unstable world—one that I had never wanted to share with them.

My entire body went electric. They were leaving. I felt heavy, dark clouds gathering over me as my sense of stability slipped through my fingers.

Rich leaped out of his chair and paced beside us. He was much taller than my father, which shifted the room's energy. Suddenly, things felt chaotic.

"Shit. The feds are doing my background check for the Livermore Labs job," Rich said. "Are they going to find out about this? Shit!" He was agitated, but my dad was a cool cucumber. He just smiled at Rich. I knew that face. It was an I'm-biting-my-tongue-here smile, but to everyone else, it looked like he was more in control than he really was. I hated that superior look he had. People who weren't hardened criminals were suckers who didn't know the score, in his view. I felt like that wasn't real life, but he had adopted this weird, defensive perspective, and I despised it.

"Don't worry. It's doubtful they'll connect us. And if they do show up here by some chance, you can just tell them the truth. You have no idea what we've done or where we are," he stated calmly. He looked at me and said, "Let's go outside to finish this conversation." We stepped out to the backyard, leaving my friends to stare at each other in disbelief.

"How will I reach you?" I squeaked.

Shreya put her arm around me, "You won't be able to, sweetie, but we'll call you every chance we get."

"I'll let your mother know what's going on," my dad said.

"But where are you going?"

"We'll head west. It's better that you don't know where, just yet."

My shock was turning to fear; I was having a hard time breathing, and I started to cry.

"What happened?" I asked.

"Someone who I used to do business with was busted. In exchange for a plea deal, the cocksucker gave them my name," he said. "It's best if we're not around for a while."

"We really shouldn't stay much longer," Shreya said.

It was dark as we said our goodbyes. I felt lost, not knowing where they were going and that they weren't going home. Ever again. They promised to call soon, and we hugged. I didn't want to let go of Blossom, her soft, warm fur my last reminder of the stable family we had pretended to be for the last three years. As they drove away, I felt a profound aloneness deep in my bones.

I was barraged with questions when I reentered the kitchen. I watched as these two parts of my life collided. The balloon had popped. I answered as simply and directly as I could. "My dad smuggles and sells pot," I said. "He's been doing it my whole life and has already spent time in prison. He doesn't want to do that again, so I guess he's gotta go."

Everyone stared at me with raised eyebrows. "Wow," Ginny replied.

"Yeah. So, it's better if you don't know much, in case anyone does show up, which hopefully won't happen. I'm sorry, Rich," I said. "I'm sorry I never told you, but it was for their safety."

Less than thirty minutes had passed, but the person my friends thought they knew was gone. The happy college student, getting ready for her corporate job, was now the heartbroken daughter of a felon.

⚡

It would be a year before I saw them again. Despite my best efforts to focus on my career and keep it together that year, the pain came out like a leaky dam. I thought drugs and alcohol would ameliorate my sense of abandonment. But eventually, after a summer of illness and a growing recognition that I was only hurting myself, I chose better.

I left an unfulfilling job, the partying, and a city where I didn't belong. I moved across the country to California, taking long beach walks, releasing my sorrow and anger in the waves, and giving myself the grace of time. There was this moment on the beach where it all hit me. Looking out at the horizon, I realized that if I wanted to connect to rootedness, it *would be* up to me, not my family. I would be the source of my strength, as steady and consistent as the ceaseless lapping of the waves.

Voices in My Head

Janell Strube

"Pray for your children's safety," commanded a voice in my head, perhaps female, perhaps even my own voice.

It was a Saturday morning in March 2019. I had just finished a poem and was rushing downstairs to print out enough copies to share in class, and keeping an eye on the clock to make sure I left in time for the seventy-mile trip down I-5 to San Diego.

Still, I knew I had to stop and obey this voice. It was as though a prescient dread had overtaken me. I took the voice to mean "pray for their physical safety."

But which child was I to pray for?

Maybe my twenty-three-year-old daughter, Aimelie, away at college in Italy? Or my thirty-two-year-old son, Anthony, living life on the edge in Florida? His home literally was a warehouse bay where he worked on cars. Could it be Alex, the girl down the street who called me Mom? My former boyfriend's five kids, barely out of their teens? They were fragile as paper lanterns in a strong wind, reeling from his sudden death in September.

I prayed for the safety of each one, then got into my car and drove slowly onto the freeway. Urgent voices have spoken to me in the past, like when I heard a man say, "He's going to hit that car." The light was green, the intersection clear, but I hesitated. Just then, two cars collided right where I should have been. Another time, when I desperately wanted to leave Florida, when I felt far from family, stressed out as a single mom, and confused over my broken marriage, I asked the universe, "Why am I here?" Meaning, why am I here in Florida? A man's voice reverberated in my head, "You are here for Anthony."

And so I stayed in Florida. Stayed for the boy who had been my foster son when he was six, who had gone home to his mother when he was eight, and who returned to foster care at the age of twelve when his mother died. I adopted Anthony when he turned sixteen.

That was sixteen years ago. Anthony was still in Florida, but I had returned to Southern California.

On I-5, traffic was easy. Beneath a cloudless blue sky, the highway scrolled like a dark-gray ribbon alongside the Pacific Ocean's sparkling indigo.

I attended class, had my poetry dissected and put back together in better form, and went for coffee with my poet friends. But throughout the day, a needle of worry that one of "my" young people might be in trouble poked at me, making it hard to concentrate.

Late in the afternoon, I left San Diego for the drive home in stop-and-go traffic. By 6:05 p.m., I-5 had eased up and was running at its usual breakneck speed between the green hills of spring to the east and the ocean to the west. It seemed that "my kids" had made it through the day, wherever in the world they were. I had heard nothing from any of them. I breathed out a huge whoosh of relief and rubbed my neck.

I should go down to the pier and give a prayer of thanksgiving.

I exited the highway, wound my way down the narrow beach-town street to the ocean, parked, and got out of my car. It was 6:27 p.m., about a half hour from sunset. I sat down on a concrete park bench and then said my prayer.

An old van pulled up beside my car. A man, an older woman, and a little boy got out to watch the sunset. The little boy was about five or so, with a round face full of freckles and a dark fringe of bangs. He saw me taking photos on my iPhone and played a game of leapfrog with an imaginary friend in front of me. He would glance at me and then back at his father sitting on the concrete bench next to mine.

The little boy had a black eye.

I stared at the father. Had this man given this little boy a black eye? If he had, what would I do? I took a deep breath and regarded the black eye with more clinical precision. In foster-care training, we were taught how to differentiate an accidental black eye from a black eye delivered at the hand of a parent. This black eye was a purple ring around the socket of the eye, with the eye socket doing its protective job, not a bruise against the cheekbone from someone's hand.

An accidental black eye. I relaxed.

The little boy continued to jump around in front of me—hoping, perhaps, that I would take his photo—and then retreated to the safety of his father.

He looked just like my son when I first met him at the children's shelter. Anthony was smaller than every child there, pale, undersized, stoic. He had been in the thirty-day shelter for more than ninety days. "All the kids here will be friendly, but Anthony will ignore you," the shelter director told my then-husband and me as we headed out to the playground to meet him. She explained how he had gone to court and asked the judge to place him in a foster home.

The playground had a jungle gym in the middle, with one little boy standing alone beside it. The other children, about six of them, swarmed around us, demanding our attention.

"Do you want to watch me ride a bike?" one asked.

"Are you here to take me home?" another asked.

Anthony hung back on the playground, regarding us with an unsmiling face and serious brown eyes in a white sea of freckles.

"Why don't you show these people what you can do on the monkey bars, Anthony?" the director asked.

He dutifully climbed up and swung carefully, perfectly, across them, his face expressionless, as though he had no hope that we might choose him. At that moment, Anthony became the son of my heart.

"We'll take him home," I said.

Water slapped against the pylons, and the smell of sea spray brought me back to the present.

I watched the little boy watching his father, and I wondered what Anthony's life would have been like if he had had a father. Would he have had to go through all the losses he did? Would he have ended up in foster care?

"Anthony already has a father," boomed a voice in my head. A heavenly father, the voice meant.

That's true, I thought. I continued snapping photos until the sun sank into the waves, then texted my son. "I'm down here watching the sunset," I typed. I sent him the three best photos I had taken. The sun, a fireball of yellow surrounded by orange that shimmered across the ocean like a line of storm clouds, the vector of sherbet bisecting my photo at a five-degree angle where the sun blinded the camera. The yellow line the sun flung across the water, skipping the waves like a wind-tossed stone. The narrow palm trees turned dark against the sky along the beach, the poles of the pier stretching toward the endless day.

"There's a little boy here who looks just like you when you were at the shelter. I'm so glad I met you, so glad you're my son. Love you." I hit send, then watched the sky continue its journey from rose to purple, the water turning orange as the sun disappeared.

I drove home.

Around ten o'clock, my son called.

"Mom," he said. "Your text message was insane."

"What do you mean?"

"I just got back from the emergency room," he said.

Three minutes after I had said my prayer of thanksgiving, on the other side of the country, at 9:30 p.m. Florida time, Anthony had climbed into a stranger's car outside his shop. This gentleman had stopped by to show off his vintage BMW. The two of them decided to take the man's car for a spin through the warehouses to see how fast it could go from zero to sixty. My son got in the passenger seat and buckled himself in.

They took off, my son filming the ride on his cell phone. On the first pass through the warehouses, my son advised the man on the direction to take. "Don't go the other way," Anthony said. "You'll hit the warehouse." They made it through the first pass. Then the man turned his car around.

"I didn't hit second gear," he said. "Let me try again."

"Whoa—what are you doing, man?" Anthony asked as the driver accelerated.

The driver lost control. The BMW skidded and crashed into the warehouse. The man died right there in the driver's seat.

Anthony unbuckled his seatbelt and kicked his way out through the shattered windshield. His physical injuries? The burn from the seatbelt that had stopped his own acceleration through the car, and lots of bruises.

"I just got back to my shop and went to look for my cell phone," he said. "It flew out the window in the accident. When I found the phone, your text was on it."

I picked up my phone to go back through my sunset photos.

Had that little boy really been down at the sunset with me?

SEARCHING FOR MY PURPLE

NICOLE ANTOINETTE LEWIS

I met my father while coming down from my first acid trip. It was the spring of 1992, and I was nineteen.

The night before, I was at my friend Heather's house in her basement with our other friends. Heather was one year older than me and wore her hair long, limp, and dirty, like the '90s grunge musicians.

Heather's basement was *lush* in purple. The chairs, lamps—*and even the walls were painted purple.* Four Siamese cats lounged around the L-shaped sofa and stared at us with peculiarity and awe. We were listening to "The Joker" by Steve Miller and *tripping balls,* a term I learned that night, which meant you were heavily hallucinating. The song was on repeat, and when it began for the third time, everything in the room got fuzzy.

I looked over at my friend Jake. Waves of rainbow hues rippled beneath his face, and his high cheekbones became more pronounced. Suddenly, I remembered the night he told me his grandfather was Cherokee. We had traded stories about our families, took swigs of Schlitz Malt Liquor forties, and bonded over our Native American ancestry. I will never forget the glow of sincerity on Jake's face when he spoke about his legacy and how confident he was about where he came from. On the other hand, I talked with uncertainty when I shared stories about my family history.

I dashed across the hall to look at my reflection in the bathroom mirror. Magenta and crimson tones danced around my dark-amber cheeks. I stood there mesmerized, staring into the mirror. I traced over the hues running through my skin, replaying my mom's and grandmother's stories about their side of the family, and I realized I didn't know much about my father's side.

I thought of Jimi Hendrix's "Purple Haze" and how, in high school, I used to create elaborate stories of how *he* was my father, because my dad wasn't in my life. I even took up guitar lessons to make it seem more convincing. It was much easier to pretend a dead rock star was my father than someone still alive who abandoned me. I fantasized about what it would be like to have a father who took me to the park, walked around with me on his shoulders—and treated me like his little princess.

Back in the room with my friends, I was fascinated by Heather's purple and blue tie-dyed T-shirt—it blended and swirled with bursts of color. I was enchanted, and purple became my obsession.

With my arms swimming toward her, I said, "I want to dive into your shirt, Heather. Can I have your shirt?"

I searched the basement for hours for that particular shade of purple. Heather had a twenty-four-pack of crayons that I rummaged through desperately, but I could not find that purple. There were magentas, plums, lavenders, and lilacs, but they all seemed to fade to black. My friends started to humor themselves by bringing different clothing from a laundry basket.

"Is this the purple?"

"What about this one?"

"Noo!" I answered in frustration, because nothing seemed to fulfill what I was seeking. *They* thought it was hysterical.

It was the break of dawn and time for me to go. I stepped into the hazy Maryland morning and walked through the tall, uncut grass, moist with dew, that felt cool against my ankles. The air was filled with the sweetness of wild honeysuckle, and the sky—electric dark indigo.

As I got into my car, I couldn't stop thinking about my father, Charles Lewis. I longed to see him right away. *But why? I hadn't seen him since I was seven in a crowded courtroom when I sat on the stand testifying against him.*

As I unlocked the key to my apartment, I recalled that day in court. He sat across from me, staring at me with disappointment as I told the judge about the weekend he had spent with us and how he pretended to be a loving father. He took me and my mom Christmas shopping, and I was elated because I had a mom *and* a dad. We were a complete family. Little did we know, he'd been casing our house to rob it. The last night he stayed with us, I saw him enter the room, check if I was awake, and then steal my grandmother's rings and necklaces from her jewelry box.

While his lawyer cross-examined me, I tried my best to avoid eye contact with him, and when we finally locked eyes, there was a disconnect. I was looking at a stranger.

Back in my room, the acid was still in full effect, and my mind was racing. If I wanted to see Charles, would he want to see me? Would he still be mad? Maybe he would make amends, and I would forgive him, and we would have the loving relationship I always dreamed of.

And then another memory flashed before my eyes. I was eight years old, sitting with my Aunt Sabrina, and she spoke words I never forgot: "Charles is not your real father."

The sun had finally risen, and my room was glowing in the golden morning light. I was consumed with one thought.

I wanted the truth.

My skin began to tremble. I called my mother. She picked it up in one ring.

"What's wrong?" she asked. "It's 6 a.m."

"Mom, I want to see Charles."

Who cares that he was a heroin addict who robbed us on Christmas Eve? I just wanted to see him. There was a long silence, and then she answered, "Why?" in a tone I had never heard her use.

"I know we haven't seen him in over twelve years, but I want to know him again," I said with urgency.

My mom was still silent. I didn't even hear her breathing.

I questioned myself: *Was Charles my father? What was my mother keeping from me?*

"Mom, did you hear me?"

Finally, after moments of silence, she said, "Charles Lewis is not your real father."

"Mom, are you high?" I asked her, which was ironic, because I was the one tripping.

"Charles is not your father," she repeated. "Your *real f*ather is a man named Leon."

My bedroom grew dark, and I looked out the window just as a cloud slowly covered the sun. "Nicole. Nicoole . . . are you there?" My mother's voice jolted me.

"Nicole, get ready. I am coming to pick you up. I have somewhere to take you. I just have to make a quick call. I will be there in twenty minutes," she said, and hung up the phone.

We drove south, heading to Washington, D.C. The streets and trees were blurry and wavy, and my head was about to explode. I felt like I was inside the painting *The Scream* by Edvard Munch.

My mom and I didn't speak during the thirty-five minutes it took to drive to the 1900 block of Q Street in Southeast. Although there were knots in my stomach and fluttering in my chest, I embraced the rollercoaster of emotions, because questions were being answered.

My mom parked right out front of the red-brick row house between two white houses. Dazed, I stared out the window before I got out of the car. My feet were wobbly as I walked up the six clay-colored concrete steps that led to the entrance. Mom was ahead of me. She opened the white screen door and knocked. A tall man with ebony-colored skin opened the door.

"Hello," I said, in an uncertain whisper.

"Hi, Nikki," he said, with a confidence that surprised me.

"How do you know my name? Do you know who I am?"

"Ask yo mama," he said in a deep voice, with a slight southern Maryland accent. He continued, "I'm yo daddy." His upbeat and laid-back demeanor threw me off guard. I stood there mystified, staring at my biological father for the first time. I traced his whole face to find myself inside his features. In his gentle and warm oval eyes, *I found my eyes.* In his smile, *I found my smile,* and in his childlike laughter, *I heard my laugh.* "Well, don't just stand there; come in," he said.

The living room was slightly dark, with hardwood floors, white antiqued couches, and turquoise walls. It was warm and welcoming. I sat down on one of the couches for a few minutes, but I don't remember having a long conversation. I was tired, overwhelmed, and coming down off LSD.

My father sensed I needed a nap and took me upstairs to his room so I could rest in his king-sized bed while he and my mom stayed in the living room. I slept for hours. It took me a minute to remember where I was when I woke. I looked out the arch-shaped window as the sun was setting. The sky was painted in fuchsias, golden orange, *and* the most *beautiful* shade of purple.

I was home.

CATCHING A BREATH

DAVEY SMITH, MD

Melbourne, Australia, January 2020
Deaths from COVID-19 worldwide: 8

On the seventh day of my vacation, the low hum of our cruise ship pulling into Melbourne Harbor vibrated my small stateroom bed and woke me up. Finally, at the relaxed point in the vacation, I woke up thinking about the albatross rookery I saw in New Zealand two days before, not about my work as a professor and infectious disease doctor—writing grants and papers, seeing patients in the clinic, and researching in the lab. Staring at the acoustic-tiled ceiling, I pleasantly remembered how when an albatross takes off for its first flight, it won't touch the ground again for four years, until it comes back to the rookery to breed.

The small bed meant that my husband, Asher, snored closer to my ear than usual, so I rolled over. Out the small porthole window, I saw no city skyline, no sunrise, no water—only a dark gray haze. Thinking that we were moving through a heavy fog in the harbor, I got up and opened the small window. I loved the cool moisture of fog, and our stuffy room needed some fresh air. Large dollops of the haze poured into the room like gray milk, and the smell of acrid smoke burned my nose. I coughed and then quickly shut the window. Asher sprung up in a fright. "Is the ship on fire?"

The ship wasn't on fire, but Australia was. Over the previous few days, I had seen on the news that because of climate change, it was hotter and drier than had ever been recorded in Australia, and large swaths of the continent were ablaze. Millions of animals were being burned alive. Smoke had obscured my first-ever view of Melbourne.

Wondering if the fires were burning close to Melbourne, I turned on the TV and found the news. Instead of giving me information about the fires, the news reporter told me about a mysterious pneumonia in China. How thousands of people had gotten sick, and some died. How the Chinese had to start building hospitals to take care of the patients. How the WHO was investigating. How it was likely a new virus.

My chest tightened. Of course it was a new virus, I thought. Probably a coronavirus, like Severe Acute Respiratory, i.e., SARS, which broke out in China in 2002. This new virus was probably the Son-of-SARS, or SARS Junior. It was going to be a problem.

Assured that the ship was not on fire, Asher was back to snoring, so I turned down the volume as the reporter speculated wildly about the new pathogen's origin. I looked out the window and still saw nothing.

How many plagues does God need to use to get their point across? I thought. I remembered when I heard about my first plague.

Middle Valley, Tennessee, 1983
Deaths from HIV in the US: 8,304

Do you remember the first time you heard of AIDS?

The first time I heard about AIDS was when I was twelve years old in Middle Valley, Tennessee. A dozen and so miles north of Chattanooga and nestled along North Chickamauga Creek under Mowbray Mountain, Middle Valley was a nice place to grow up in the late twentieth century. For a boy in his early adolescence, there were forests and creeks to explore. There were robins, cardinals, and blue jays in the spring, and squirrels all year. I liked to fish in the fall, and I was fascinated by bugs—flip beetles, green dragonflies, katydids, praying mantises, lightning bugs. I kept a growing collection of discarded snake skins, deer antlers, and sun-bleached turtle shells on my windowsill. I rode my bike on the dirt road by my house with Keith, the kid who lived down the street, for hours every afternoon until it got dark. Back and forth never seemed boring, and there never seemed like there was enough time to get it all in.

One such night, I saw the porch light blink. It was Mom's signal that dinner was ready and that it was time for me to set the table. My friend Keith peeled off to go back to his house, and I pedaled fast to our house's back door, jumping off my bike to make a leap onto the stoop—my go-to move. Sometimes I made it, but most of the time, I didn't. That evening, my dog Snuffy distracted me by barking as I approached, and I tumbled knees-first into the gravel. I jumped up, brushed myself off, and went inside. The smell of spaghetti and burned bread filled the house. "Your knee is bleeding on the carpet," my mother said, when she saw me. "Go wash it and put on a bandage."

I had acquired a lot of scars in my adventures by falling out of trees, wrecking my bike, jumping off tire swings into the swimming hole but sometimes missing, or simply tripping over my own feet. My mother was convinced that I did not believe in gravity. My father just said I was clumsy like him. They were both right.

Being the end of July and before next month's paycheck, my mom, a fifth-grade teacher who did not get paid in the summer, had made the spaghetti with zucchini instead of hamburger meat. It was not my favorite. My little brother was already carrying dinner plates bigger than his head to the table. He loved spaghetti, so long as the noodles didn't touch the sauce.

The *NBC Nightly News* played in the background of supper. My brother ate his sauceless noodles first. I kicked him under the table to make him kick back. He did not take the bait.

A menacing male voice from the TV proclaimed that a new cancer or virus was killing homosexual men in New York and San Francisco. It was a "gay plague." I acted as if I were not paying attention, but I listened closely to every word that the disembodied voice said. I was too young to understand what "gay" or "plague" meant, and I had never been to a city bigger than Chattanooga, but I knew that big cities like New York and San Francisco were where people lived who could not live in Middle Valley.

That night, I couldn't sleep. *What was a virus? How did someone get it? Was it already in Middle Valley somewhere? Was I going to get it?* I slipped out of bed with my flashlight. The hallway outside my parents' room was dark, and I could hear my father's snoring from behind their bedroom door. I crept down the hallway, making sure to avoid the creaky spot on the floor. I went to our bookcase in the living room, where we had a set of the new 1982 *Encyclopedia Britannica.* I sat cross-legged on the floor with the large brown book in my lap as I read about viruses.

I learned that a virus is a very small package of proteins and genetic particles called nucleic acids. Each kind of virus targeted a particular type of cell, such as a white blood cell, a liver cell, or a lung cell. A virus was like a parasite, eating the cells from the inside out. Viruses reminded me of the big, swollen ticks on our dog Snuffy, a cocker spaniel mix who loved to chase rabbits and squirrels through the East Tennessee thickets, which was also one of my favorite things. It was my job to brush Snuffy's coat, pick out the ticks, and either squish them between my fingernails or drop them in rubbing alcohol. I would toss the big fat ones on the ground and step on them with a bloody splat. I was protecting my dog from blood-sucking invaders.

I knew the ticks needed to drink Snuffy's blood so they could feed their babies. In the same way, the viruses needed to feed off the cells so they could make copies of themselves, like their babies. Once made, these baby viruses spread to infect other cells in the body. Depending on the type of virus and the cells that it infected, the viral infection could cause liver damage or pneumonia. My fascination grew, and I looked up and learned each term I did not know––gene, nucleic acid, protein, pneumonia. It was like the time I got grounded for watching *The Shining*. I could not turn away.

The *Encyclopedia Britannica* also said that most of the time, the body's immune system could recognize when a virus was reproducing in the body and that it would make specialized proteins, called antibodies, that could kill the virus and its progeny virions in response. This was the reason why the common cold lasted about a week. So, to survive, viruses had to move from one person to another, then another, in quick succession, like with a sneeze or cough or handshake. The thought of this made me want to wash my hands, which soon became an obsession.

The next Sunday, my uncle, who was also the preacher of our family's small fundamentalist church, preached other theories. He must have heard the same news report that we heard. From the elevated pulpit he said, as if he were reading directly from John 3:16, that AIDS was the way God told us that he was unhappy with how we were acting. That gay people did not have God's grace. My uncle was my authority on God, so I believed him—AIDS was sent from God to punish gay people. Not only could a virus kill you, but it could also send you to hell.

The problem was, I was in love with Keith.

Scars

Laura L. Engel

For five decades, I suffered from an immense jagged scar, and it was invisible to all.

In 1967, I was a pregnant teen facing no support from the father, a boy I had believed when he said he loved me. Nine months later, I was forced to relinquish my newborn son for a closed adoption in a maternity home for unwed mothers in New Orleans. I secretly grieved the loss of my firstborn son for fifty years. But in 2016, when he and I were brought together through the remarkable science of DNA, my life exploded in joyful Technicolor. The warmth of that reunion cracked my heart wide open.

"I thought of you every day and wondered if you were happy and loved," I told him.

"I have had a very good life and thought of you, too. I worried that if I found you, you wouldn't want me in your life." I cringed. I knew how frightened I had been about him finding me but had not realized how brave he had been to face the fear of rejection from the mother who had left him.

Gathering my courage, I whispered, "I always wanted you in my life, but I worried you would hate me."

"I never hated you. How could I? You gave me life."

Those words alone brought me a type of peace I had not felt since leaving my baby.

After our reunion, I tearfully confessed to my adult children that there was a brother they did not know about. Then, I began the dreaded task of telling other family and friends that I had held this secret from them. Despite everyone's shock, I was met with tremendous support and care. Why had I been so fearful? I had privately remained grief-stricken and wary of rejection like that frightened young girl in the 1960s, even though I was now a much older, wiser woman. And then, a remarkable thing happened as I shared the story of my secret son; I began to heal. At last, I felt whole again. My son was magically back, I had willingly exposed my scar, and the people in my life had showered me with understanding.

Each morning, I woke up with a smile on my face. All four sons I had birthed were accounted for in my life, and all four were happy, healthy, and treasured. Multiple family trips back and forth across the country to visit each other resulted in beautiful "firsts" for all of us. I met three new grandchildren, celebrated my adopted son's birthday for the first time at fifty, and watched all my sons celebrate together on Christmas Eve. My family welcomed this unknown son and his family into our lives without hesitation. Although two thousand miles stretched between our home and my eldest son's, we talked often, resulting in hours of conversations, laughs, and tears—and always, the wonder that we had finally met.

"Can you tell me more about when you were a young girl and about my brothers?" he asked. I loved showing him photos and sharing old family stories.

"Now it's your turn. Tell me more about you growing up. Were you happy? What were your adoptive parents like?" I soaked up every word, heartbroken I had missed those years and simultaneously wishing I could thank the people who had loved and raised my son.

I had doubted I would ever see his face or hear his voice, and yet, within days of our reunion, he called me Mom. Each time he did, it filled me up, but still, there was that prick of worry because this glorious time seemed too good to be true. A friend advised me, "Live in the moment. Enjoy this remarkable reunion and all the good things coming from it."

From that day forward, I concentrated on the miracle of our reunion. I let my heart expand. I smiled and laughed more than I ever had. I wanted to tell the world my son had found me. Just knowing each night where all my children were calmed my soul. All the puzzle pieces had fallen into the right places, and I felt gratitude every day—well, every hour.

Four and a half years is a blink of an eye in the long tapestry of life. My family was complete for one thousand, six hundred and forty-two days.

One evening, my phone rang as I chopped vegetables for a stir fry. My oldest grandson's photo lit up the screen, and I happily grabbed it.

"Hi, dear! How are you?" I was delighted that this young man, who had only known me for such a short time, felt comfortable enough to text and chat with me, his new grandmother.

"Grammy." His voice was quivering. He hesitated.

Sensing something was wrong, I quickly asked if he was okay.

"Grammy." He began again, hesitated, then spoke. "Dad is gone."

"Gone where?" My grandson tearfully explained that my son, my firstborn, was dead. My son had taken his own life.

My grandson's father, the son who I had mourned for five decades, was gone, and this time it was forever. As I crumbled, folding into myself, trembling, horrified, a long wail came from my deepest core.

Confused, I grappled with this new reality. I needed to comfort my grandson, but words left me, except for "Why? Why God, why?" When I think back to those days, I only remember my shaking hands, my aching chest, and more tears than I thought any human being could cry. A dense fog clouded my brain, and the absolute heaviness I felt in my body would not lift. I forgot to eat or drink. I couldn't speak without breaking down. The torturous long flight across the country to mourn along with my grandchildren remains a blur.

In the past, whenever I heard of someone losing a child, a shudder would run through me. How would those gutted parents live on? Surely, they would never smile or laugh again. Now, I was one of those parents. I had only imagined the grief, never the anger that accompanied it. I closed myself off from the world, alone in my bedroom, alternately wailing and raging, then pleading with the Universe. "Why did you let us find each other only for me to lose him again?"

Not only had I lost my son for a second and final time, but it was in such a way that I simply could not wrap my head around it. I lost my voice, unable to speak the words of my son's death. I began stuffing the pain down, privately suffering just as I had after leaving him as an infant.

I remained in deep and private mourning, but life was slowly returning to normal, and I woke one morning aware that I was learning to live with this grave loss. Life would be different. I would once again hold my son's birth card to my heart and sob on his birthday, just as I had over the long years of not knowing where he was. I will forever miss his voice calling me Mom.

Putting together the lessons I had learned in the past five years, I stopped holding in my pain. I began to speak my truth. I remembered finding innate kindness and goodness in people when I had spoken about the shame and grief of surrendering my son all those years ago. Hadn't this taught me that relief is enormous when we speak from our hearts, and the love and support we receive back is incredible? Light slowly streamed back into my life, and I could glimpse gratitude for all the good that was left.

The first time I spoke to a group about my son's suicide, I felt naked and exposed. I broke down, wondering if I had done the right thing. Afterward, I received emails from mothers thanking me for having enough courage to speak of my loss. One mother said I may have saved her daughter. She had worried about her daughter harming herself. Now, she was determined to be proactive and seek help for her.

Helping others lit up my heart, and I began to talk freely about the tragic experience of losing my son twice, once to adoption and then to suicide. I found solace in the fact my son and I had found and held onto each other for almost five years. His suicide was only part of our story. The most powerful lesson for me was that you do not have to suffer alone in your grief. There are angels here on earth who will guide and help you, just for the asking. Thanks to those scars, I will strive to be one of those angels.

My Father's Moon

Lenore Greiner

My grief was thick. The finality of death and all of its heaviness loomed over me. How would I be able to live in a world without my father? I could barely get through a day without randomly bursting into tears when hearing certain songs or when I remembered myself as a child placing my tiny hand in his.

About a month into my grief, I sat down for my regular morning meditation. Within a few minutes, a swirling warmth washed over my body. I felt as if I was no longer alone. Even stranger, it was as if my father was there with me, wrapping his arms around the pain and lifting me out of grief. Then he began speaking. I couldn't see him, but I heard him within my heart, half in feelings, half in words.

I placed my pen on paper and wrote down one word that came to me—then another and another, never knowing the next. "Mom's okay—I watch her."

But it wasn't just Mom; he had thoughts on his grandchildren and his friends. Soon, sentences flowed from my pen, filling my journal pages. When I stopped to read, I shook my head, astounded. This can't be real. Am I really listening to my dad? Or is my grief making the fantastical real? My heart sank. He probably wasn't there.

A few days later, my anguish evolved into the physical. One day, out of the blue, a cruel pain stabbed me in the back between my shoulder blades. Seeing me wince, my husband, Rob, asked, "What's wrong?"

"It's that random pain again. Don't know why."

I twisted my tense shoulders. "It comes and goes. Nothing I do stops it, and it's getting worse."

I sought treatment from the capable Dr. Anika, an Indian Ayurvedic medical doctor. In her office, draped with sari fabric, she took one look at me.

"It's a heart chakra issue—a broken heart."

"Oh, my dad just died."

"Come, lay down here."

I lay face down on a massage table as she lowered the lights, lit incense, and filled the room with a slow, melodic Sanskrit chant for a father who had died. Her hands expertly prepared a warm medicinal oil infused with herbs for a daughter grieving her father. She dug in with strong fingers after running ribbons of the warm oil up and down my spine. A tight, pained breath escaped me.

"You're full of knots."

As she spoke, a chill breeze slipped over my bare legs. Then, that similar rush of love cascaded over me.

Dad.

I felt his presence just beyond my shoulder in the corner of the room as his love for me unfurled. Recognizing this familiar wave of emotion from my meditations, this time, I surrendered to the intensity and accepted his gift. The darkened room seemed to expand to contain the immensity of his love. The scent of the incense grew stronger, and the sacred music seemed to vibrate. My breath calmed.

"Oh, there's a presence here," said Dr. Anika.

She feels him, too.

"My dad. He comes to me sometimes."

I couldn't bring myself to share how, since his death, I heard his voice during morning meditation, filling my journal with his words. But soon, my knots released, and I felt my mysterious stabbing pain fade away. As her fingers circled over my loosened muscles, she said, "Hmm, you're like a baby now. Thank him for his help."

Then I heard my dad say, "Just doing my job."

His common saying to us kids while growing up, after we'd thanked him for something.

"Oh," said Dr. Anika, "now he's saying that he'll love you forever."

What? I was shaken with shock; tears sprang into my eyes.

"That's exactly what I whispered into his ear before leaving his hospital room," I choked. "On the night he died."

Her validating Dad's presence the moment he flew in was a profound gift. Simply knowing that she heard him, too, sent a flood of relief through my body. Quicksilver-fast messages flooded in. *Don't dwell on his death, his illness, with such deep mourning. Dwell upon the great things he did. Dwell upon my own family and my happy future.*

"Then, at your funeral," I heard him say, "your loved ones will feel love and joy for you."

"How long has it been since your father died?" Dr. Anika's question snapped me back onto her massage table. Wrapped in a sheet, my body filled with serenity, I rose with great slowness.

"Well, he died on January 12."

As I wiped away tears on the sheet, she shuffled her calendar.

"Today is February 14. Exactly one month. You can do a puja for him, a special ritual to pray for his peace. Do this up to forty-five days after his passing to help with his transition."

Apparently, it takes time for the dead to get used to being dead.

In India, I had experienced the pujas, sacred rites redolent of incense, tiny flames, abundant flowers, tinkling bells, and drapes of resplendent silk. Her idea resonated deeply since pujas always created an intense peace and closeness to God. Both Rob and I had fought boredom during the masses of our childhoods, reciting rote chants and prayers. As adults, we abandoned Catholicism's black-and-white dogma. After learning in India that all paths lead to God, I

drew closer to Eastern practices, the simplicity of Buddhism's mindful meditation, and the intensity of Hinduism's devotion to God.

"You know, my dad always said that India was his favorite trip. We both loved
it there."

"Ah, the forty-third day after his death is very auspicious. A full moon
will rise in the evening, and that day commemorates Saraswati, the goddess of
knowledge, music, and the arts."

"Perfect. My dad was a musician, and I'm a writer."

"Pray for him and let his good karma become tenfold to help him through
his transition. And do charity on his behalf."

"Yes, I've donated to the hospice where I'm getting grief counseling."

On the forty-third day after Dad's passing, I dressed in my finest Indian silks
and entered a Hindu temple. Rob and our thirty-two-year-old son, Michael,
agreed to join me. They suffered, too. Perhaps this may help them. A Hindu
priest in his thirties, Kamal, greeted us, wearing a warm smile and pure white
Indian clothes. He asked us to wash our hands and sit cross-legged on a carpet on
the white marble floor. A pantheon of Hindu deities stood over us, each inside
their own marble niche, arrayed in floral garlands, lavish silks, and gold tinsel.
At their feet, offering baskets overflowed.

I gave Kamal a framed photo of Dad smiling. He placed it with great respect
upon a brass tray laden with marigolds and roses, incense, holy water, coconut,
rice, crimson powder, a lit oil lamp, and a plate of Indian sweets. My body
relaxed as our resplendent puja began.

"Now, we will honor your father," said Kamal in a soft voice. Overseen by the
gods, he gently chanted in Sanskrit while purifying us with wafts of incense and
sprinklings of holy water. Then he waved a tray of tiny oil-lamp flames around
our heads. A stillness crept in, followed by a sense of unfolding love, like a pink
cloud expanding above our heads.

"Let's chant the sacred mantra, Shanti Om, for peace, for our peace, and for
his peace."

He placed a tilak, a crimson powder mark, between our eyebrows.

"For concentration."

He even placed a tilak on Dad's forehead in the photo, and I liked to think that he liked that. Kamal placed a marigold on my palm, asking me to chant Shanti Om. After Rob and Michael did the same, he put our flowers on Dad's tray.

Following Dr. Anika's instruction, I prayed "to let his good karma become tenfold to get him through his transition." I gazed over to Dad's picture and found his face aglow as if backlit, giving him life.

He's here with us. He's happy. I floated in gratitude.

A deep calm engulfed my body, and my spine tingled. I turned to Rob and Michael, finding their faces incandescent with peace.

Concluding the puja, Kamal waved the tray of dancing flames around my father, symbolizing how God drives away the darkness. My throat caught a sob. When we stood up, Kamal shared the Indian sweets as a prasad or gift from God. I presented my Dakshina, a temple offering, and we took photos. I shot a photo of Dad smiling from his overflowing tray.

As we left the temple, the full moon's huge face hung in the sky like a giant theatrical backdrop.

"It's my father's moon!"

The next morning, my father's voice resonated within me, true and real. Expanding gusts of overwhelming love flooded my body, bringing on more tears.

"Honor your father and your mother," he said. "Yes, I'm smiling," he added. "It feels so good to be here, getting used to it. I'm very peaceful and understand so much now. There is so much love."

I quickly scratched his words into my journal. Then, I put down my pen, savoring his presence, and I felt a truth hang in the air.

There is no death, only the beginning of a new life.

Saving Magdi

Ruth Magdi Hargrove

The lobotomizing buzzer unlocked the steel door to the attorney waiting room inside the detention center. The door auto-locked behind me. I handed the guard a slip for my twenty-nine-year-old Cameroonian client. The guard barked, "David Moussa," and I peered down a corridor—the portal to the prison bowels. David, dark-skinned and slight, materialized at the far end, his hands behind his back as if handcuffed, shadowed by an armed guard. He'd committed no crime. He'd fled 8,000 miles to ask for asylum at our border. Instead, Immigration and Customs Enforcement, otherwise known as ICE, shackled, handcuffed, and delivered him here. One hundred and twenty days ago.

His posture erect, David looked straight ahead, impossibly gathering shards of dignity, despite the neon orange jumpsuit, the white tube socks, and the slap his cheap Walmart shower shoes made against the echoing tile.

His face blurred, and I time traveled backward eighty years—to 1940. I imagined seeing my then-sixteen-year-old father step off the *SS Samaria* at Ellis Island. He held his Deutsche Reich passport. On its cover, two eagles grasped swastikas in their talons, and a giant red "J" for "Juden" bled large.

I shook my head to clear the image.

Just then, the guard deposited David in a tomb-sized room. David was clean-shaven, with red-ringed eyes too old for his face. I explained I would be his asylum lawyer and began, "Why did you leave Cameroon?"

"Security forces shot me."

"Why?"

"The dictator, Biya, has tried to erase us since before I was born. We were the minority, and if we opposed him, the police would arrest us, beat us, or kill us. He sent the military to hunt boys over fifteen. Each day when we woke up, we turned on the radio to hear another dead body had been left on the roadside.

"One day, my friend Joseph, who ran the radio station, announced a protest. A thousand youths came out. We sang 'We want peace' and 'stop killing youth' as we marched. Military trucks filled with army soldiers wearing black masks and carrying big guns surrounded us and started shooting."

David scraped his chair back and pulled up the left leg of his jumpsuit to reveal the scar from the bullet that pierced his knee. "My shoe filled with blood, my leg collapsed, and I crawled to the side of the road. Fourteen died. Two were my friends."

He said other friends dragged him to the hospital. Lying on a gurney with his eyes closed, David did not see the photographer from the radio station who snuck into the hospital to take his photo. The photo went up instantly on the radio station's Facebook page, captioned, "Youths wounded with live bullets. One of which is David Moussa, Atwed neighborhood."

On his gurney, David's cell rang, and a friend yelled, "Soldiers are in your house!"

"My blood ran cold," David told me. They knew his name and where he lived. His friends dragged him off his gurney and into the jungle moments before the soldiers stormed inside the hospital.

"Soldiers took revenge for the protest, burning houses, killing, attacking the doctors who treated us. Everyone but the very old fled to the jungle. Babies and mothers. Pregnant women. We lived there for a year. But eventually, the military tracked us and shot us out of hiding."

As David spoke, the face of my father's cousin, Magdi, appeared in my mind's eye, as she was in the one photo I'd seen of her—a young girl smiling into the camera. Short brown hair and big brown eyes. She reminded me of me. Dressed like a tomboy, a dreamy look in her eyes. She had her whole life ahead of her.

Magdi and my father were born nine months apart to sisters in Vienna, raised more like siblings than cousins. When the Nazis occupied Vienna, Magdi's family fled, only to be trapped in Romania, where they hid in the forest. Nazis captured Magdi and forced her, with 998 other teenage girls, on a transport to Auschwitz. As my father aged, Magdi remained nineteen, dead in the dust of Auschwitz. He remembered her in my middle name and then never spoke of her again.

Back in the detention center, I heard David exhale softly. I realized I was with him in this room because he had been caught in the same type of violence and hatred that had consumed my father and Magdi. Violence and hatred I'd recently felt blowing in my own world. I watched neo-Nazis on TV, goosestepping down Charlottesville streets, bearing tiki torches and bellowing, "Jews will not replace us!" Not long after that, a former law student of mine, now an asylum lawyer, called me.

"Professor. My agency needs volunteer lawyers for imprisoned asylum seekers. Lives are on the line."

"I'd like to help, but I've never tried an asylum case in my life."

"If you don't take David's case, he'll have no voice."

From that moment forward, I was a novice with a death penalty case. If the judge denied David asylum, ICE would deport him to Cameroon. He would be hand-delivered to the men who had been hunting him for two years.

I had four weeks until the hearing, and I didn't even have a real office. I had a triangle desk wedged into the corner of our family room and a printer that labored noisily before giving agonizing birth to a single sheet of paper. I researched frantically and learned that the law entitled David to asylum. But the judge would grant it only if she believed him. This was a trial of credibility. I needed corroboration from other witnesses.

Two weeks before the trial, I flew across the country to meet with Joseph and a few other Cameroonian refugees who could corroborate David's story. In a sweltering one-room apartment, I took witness statements. I listened to each witness speak about the massacre, and then I wove their memories into one chronological story and filed my prehearing brief.

The day of David's hearing, I sat in the courtroom, drenched in fear. David sat next to me; he hadn't slept all night, hoping it was his last night in this prison.

The judge took the bench. The government lawyer moved to exclude all witness statements. In a second, the judge granted the motion—witness statements gone.

I felt tackled from behind. Our case had been ripped out by the roots. The judge wouldn't see the corpses riddled with bullets from the same guns that shot David. She wouldn't hear the photographer confess he'd turned David into a human sacrifice to prove Cameroon's atrocities. And only an hour into the remnants of our case, the judge silenced David's testimony. "We have to stop, due to time. Return in six weeks." David looked back at me, sucker-punched, as the guard returned him to the prison bowels.

I navigated my way out of the prison, my glasses fogging as tears dripped below the frames. When I crawled inside my ancient Hyundai in the prison parking lot, my powerlessness boiled into hysteria. I'd lost the life-saving evidence. David would die.

Six weeks later, the trial resumed. The government lawyer put David on the stand to be cross-examined. In an effort to suggest David was lying, the lawyer quoted from an excluded witness statement that differed from David's testimony. I objected, pointing out that counsel couldn't cross with statements he'd asked to be kept out of evidence.

The lawyer bleated, "I prepared my whole cross with those statements."

"Objection sustained. No cross on that issue."

The lawyer deflated.

With both sides presented, it was time for the judge to rule. "This is all about credibility," she intoned. "On the one hand, the respondent was the only witness in his case, and that weighs against him." My breath became shallow, and my chest tightened. The judge became a human pendulum, suspending David between life and death. "On the other hand, one witness, if believed, can prove his case." The pendulum swung back. But: "There are some inconsistencies in his account."

Finally, "But his testimony was detailed in ways that suggest its authenticity." The pendulum stopped. "Respondent is entitled to a grant of asylum." David and I locked eyes. I exhaled a breath I had been holding for months. His life was saved.

I asked David how he could recall so many details—the details that saved his life. He said, "I had to memorize it to tell my children the story of what happened to me."

Two days later, David walked out of the prison. He got a green card, began working, got his own apartment, and he's getting married. He jokes he will name all his children after me. I hope he names one after Magdi. To raise her from the dust of Auschwitz. And to keep her alive.

A Spark of Madness

Kathy Pease

I heard Carter's heavy boots thumping up the stairs. With a creak and then the slam of the weathered screen door, he shuffled into our miniature kitchen and settled in a wooden straight-backed chair. The frown on his face, his grease-smeared jeans, and his scraped elbow set the tone.

"We're gonna have to get a new car, babe. I can work on the Corvair to keep it going while I'm home, but when I'm in Vietnam, you'll be in some new city and must have reliable transportation. I know we wanted to save some money, but a car payment is going to be a necessity."

The chants of the war protestors marching down our street diverted my attention as I glanced out the window. Like them, we questioned the wisdom of the war. We had fallen in love in college, and after a blissful eight months of dating, Carter's father was injured in a tractor accident, and Carter left school to put in the spring crops. He lost his student deferment and, faced with the prospect of being drafted into the army, he elected to join the navy.

Three months later, Carter was in boot camp, and we had a year's separation while I completed my teaching credential. We were still in the honeymoon phase of our four-month marriage. Our backgrounds were so similar: hardworking families trying to keep afloat with a house full of kids. There was no money for college, so we'd both had campus jobs squeezed in between classes. Budgeting was part of our DNA; save the coupons, lick the Green Stamps. It was all we knew.

><

On that dreary Sunday morning, we drove our Corvair thirty miles into San Francisco to look for a replacement. We stopped at Ford and Chevy dealerships and examined new and used cars. We heard the spiel from each enthusiastic salesperson and saw a couple of cars that would do, but everything about them was basic: no-frills, beige, and disappointing. They were practical and fit our budget, but without even discussing it, we both knew we needed more.

On a whim, we stopped at the Pontiac dealer. Ed, the salesman, proceeded to show us a LeMans and a used Bonneville. When he learned I was a teacher and Carter was in the navy, his eyes lit up. "OK, really, the sky's the limit then with our great financing packages. Let me get a list of a few cars you might be interested in. In the meantime, I'll show you what we just got in. It's an absolute beauty."

We walked out the door and saw a metallic brown 1969 GTO. The shiny new car, the color of coffee right out of the pot, drew us in with the strength of a powerful magnet.

"Now that's a car!" Carter almost swooned. "I bet this baby can really go!"

The salesman's smile broadened. "Well, this car will definitely get you there, Carter! It has a 400 cubic inch, 350 horsepower V-8 engine, an automatic transmission, and the smoothest, most powerful ride you'll ever take! You can't really appreciate this car without driving it. Why don't you take her for a spin? The freeway exit is two blocks down this street. Just for grins, see what she can do."

Ed handed Carter the keys and walked back to the showroom with a spring in his step. Carter glanced at me and grinned as if to say, "Are we really doing this?" I looked at the car again. "Let's go!" We cautiously opened the doors, not wanting to damage anything on this precious gem. Ed had called it a test drive, but we were actually leaving the zone of good judgment as we sat on the rich, tawny gold leather-like seats. I felt like a queen! This car combined elegance and pizzazz. The new-car aroma filled our lungs as I slowly ran my hands over the chocolate-brown dash. This was a muscle car, and when I glanced at Carter, all I saw was James Dean. My heart pounded. I couldn't stop smiling. Carter turned the key, and we heard, "Ba-room! Ba-room!" It did not sound like our Corvair. We looked at each other and laughed. In all of our twenty-two years, we had never been in a car like this.

We entered the freeway just as the sun burst through the San Francisco clouds, and Carter put his foot on the gas. The immense engine accelerated, and we flew down the interstate. This car took us to another plane. I'd like to say that Carter went off the deep end and lost his ability to make prudent decisions, but I have to say, I was right with him. Whatever magic they put in that car that morning, Carter and I were under its spell. The fact that we would soon be separated again, that the country was going to hell with this war, and that our budget was tight didn't enter our minds. If even for a moment, the weight had been lifted from our young shoulders.

At some point, Carter took a freeway exit, turned on the overpass, and returned to the dealership. We waved Ed over, still in the afterglow of that otherworldly experience. I'm not sure what happened next, but when we left Ed an hour or so later, we had sold our Corvair and bought that beautiful GTO. We also had a new payment that we would make every month for the next five years.

When we drove our car home to Oregon that first Christmas, we pulled into my folks' driveway, and Carter revved the engine. Suddenly, my mom, dad, brother, and sister appeared on the porch. I know my folks were happy to see us, but the sight of that expensive, fire-breathing dragon of a car set them back. They thought we had better judgment; they thought we had common sense. The faces of my siblings lit up. They raised their fists and shouted "YES!" almost in unison and then, "Can we have a ride?" When Carter left me for his three cruises to Vietnam, that GTO never let me down.

THE RING

HEATHER M. BERBERET

"**M**y mom wants to email you. Is that OK?" Kevin asked.

This was the man who, two years earlier, had replied, before I could even ask my question, "Yes, I would be happy to be your sperm donor." In what universe would I, could I, say no to an email from his mother?

It appeared within minutes.

"Hi! I'm Cecile, Kevin's mom. It's OK if you don't reply to this or don't ever want to talk to me, but I just wanted you to know that I've claimed little Ryan as my thirteenth grandbaby and am adding a diamond for her to my family ring. Thanks! Cecile."

My daughter, "Little Ryan," had been born five weeks early. As a result, I had to leave her in the hospital when she was two days old. Leaking milk and puffed up like a cabbage from fluid retention, I was a mess and completely undone by her message. Through the tears, I wrote back,

"Cecile, I am so glad you wrote, and I'm overwhelmed. Yes, of course, you are her grandmother."

When Kevin agreed to be our donor, my wife and I knew that he and his husband, Philip, would become a central part of our lives. But the possibility of a new, extended family hadn't even occurred to me. Cecile had no obligation to contact me that day or any day. She reached out to people she had never met to claim us as her own, because her heart was that big and family that important.

Kevin's siblings and their children also welcomed us into their lives, although introductions weren't always easy, even within the family. During a visit, we were hanging in the hot tub, and Kevin's six-year-old niece asked me, her little face clouded with confusion, "So, are you my aunt?" and even I felt awkward trying to describe our connection. But not once did Cecile appear self-conscious or concerned about who we were to each other. On rare occasions during which she felt the need to be a little circumspect, she would introduce my wife and me as her daughters-in-law and Ryan as Kevin's daughter. But far more frequently, she would respond as she did the first time she and Kevin's dad, Doug, came to San Diego after Ryan was born. Doug's Alzheimer's had reached an advanced stage by then, and he was often confused by new people.

When he asked Cecile who we were, she shouted across the living room, "That's Heather and Ryan. Ryan is your granddaughter. Heather is her mother. Kevin gave Heather his sperm." Her blunt declaration shocked me speechless, but that was Cecile. She didn't hold anything back. Over time, I got used to her "Kevin is their sperm donor" announcement.

It hasn't always been simple, this family-by-choice thing. I've worried about overstepping and understepping, about assuming a level of welcome that didn't exist and ignoring one that did. I've been careful not to create any conflict, afraid of messing with the good thing we had going, while also knowing full well that it would take a Titanic-sized event to sever it. But Cecile encouraged me to settle into our relationship like she did everything else, boldly and without fuss.

Things felt clear with her; we fell into a simple connection born from our appreciation for the gifts we gave each other. I made it possible for one of her beloved children to have his own child, and to that child, she gave a grandmother and extended family. Without the complexities of also partnering with him, Cecile and I were privileged to have no expectations to meet in each other, no fantasies to fulfill.

Ryan and I made only one trip to visit her without Kevin. On a day trip to the Olympic Peninsula, she talked about her life as we drove along the old-growth forest-lined roads. About growing up in Saskatchewan, then meeting and marrying Doug; about early motherhood and the challenges of caring for young children with a disabled husband who ignored his disability to the greatest extent possible; about how she continued on alone after his passing. While I cherish that day for the family history that Ryan could claim as her own, most precious to me was coming to know Cecile, not as Ryan's grandmother or my quasi-mother-in-law, but as a woman with an extraordinary spirit and the life to go with it.

On that trip, she gave Ryan her fragile Belleek coffee cup. Cream-colored with tiny hand-painted shamrocks, made from eggshell-thin porcelain, Cecile had carefully brought it back from Ireland to replace the one her mother had given her, which had broken. For Ryan's big eighth-grade family-history project that school year, she turned to Cecile and her family for information, writing about Ireland and her uncle's memory of watching the lunar rover drive across the moon for the first time, knowing that it was his father, Ryan's grandfather Doug, who helped design it.

During the 2020 COVID lockdown, Cecile's health began to fail.

"I'm tired of being alone," she told me on the phone. "I want to be with Doug." I felt both honored and terrified by her vulnerability with me.

"We will miss you terribly," I replied. "Is there anything we can do to make this easier for you?"

"No," she said, in the same stubborn tone she used when she swore at the fruit vendor at Pike Place market because he "used the Lord's name in vain" when he called those the "best g-damned oranges!"

"I've made up my mind," she continued. "You have each other and will be fine. I love you all, but I don't want to be here anymore."

I took a deep breath, my heart pounding with fear that I would say the wrong thing and not meet her in this moment in the way she needed or that I would in some way fail and betray the rest of her family.

"Cecile, are you thinking of hurting yourself?" I asked tentatively.

"Of course not; that would be a sin! No, I'm just ready for God to take me."

Immediately on the heels of my relief at the absence of suicidality came a new anxiety. What do I say back?

When I was twenty-one, I discovered my college roommate after she had deliberately taken an entire bottle of Tylenol. She survived, but the experience taught me that, ultimately, we have to choose to live or die. Despite her family's constant presence and care of her, Cecile was eighty-nine years old and felt isolated while living in constant pain. If anyone had a right to be ready to move on to the next adventure, it was her. I don't know who else she spoke to about her longing, but I felt the responsibility of her trust.

"It's alright," I said, deciding on the truth. "It's alright to want to go."

I felt a new heartache, one I had not experienced with the illness of a loved one before. While Cecile and I met because of Kevin, I believe that if our paths had crossed for another reason, because we were neighbors, went to the same church, or played in the same canasta club, we still would have been friends. The extraordinary circumstances of our meeting only gave our friendship greater meaning. More than neighbors, more than card buddies, more than an uncomfortable obligatory acquaintance, I chose to become family because I came to love her.

When she passed a few weeks later, my grief flowed through me in a clear, pure stream of sadness. I didn't have a lifetime of unmet expectations, disappointments, or misunderstandings to sort through. Our relationship was, to a great degree, simple. And therefore, so was my grief. For fourteen years, this extraordinary woman chose to gather us under her sometimes-shocking and sometimes-hilarious but always-protective wing. I felt, feel, her absence acutely.

About a month after the funeral, Kevin emailed me to let me know that the women of the family had decided to give me Cecile's grandmother's ring, the one in which Ryan's diamond was the last to be added. I told him how thoughtful that was and that I would keep it safe for Ryan.

"No," he wrote back. "It's not for Ryan. They want *you* to have it." As they have done so many times, Cecile's family again took my breath away with their generosity and grace. They aren't perfect. Like all families, they have made mistakes, learned hard lessons, and lived through sorrows that may never heal.

But even if Cecile and Doug had discovered the secret formula for the perfect family, it wouldn't have mattered to me.

That circle of gold, swirling with tiny sparkling stones that catch whatever light is available, each diamond flaring in its turn, represents the bonds that Cecile created and cultivated throughout her adult life. Of the twenty-one stones, each representing one of Cecile and Doug's children or grandchildren, there isn't one for me. I'm pretty sure giving it to me offered a simple solution to the complex problem of one ring and many women. But I hope it also means they witnessed Cecile's connection with me. We are family by choice, so wearing it has become sacramental, an outward sign of inward grace.

ARE TWO WEEKS ENOUGH?

SAADIA ALI ESMAIL

I recently met a boy—not just any boy, but someone who is a potential prospect for me in an arrangement, an arrangement for a marriage. As a first-generation Pakistani American Muslim, I grew up on Long Island in a family strict about culture and traditions. Boyfriends and dating were a no-no. It was an unspoken rule that I would marry someone my parents approved of. That's how it had always been: those who had dared to do otherwise had been practically disowned, their names no longer spoken in our household. And yet I knew my parents would give me the final choice to say yes or no. Such was the marriage between our roots and our adopted American home.

For the past three years since I graduated from college, I have busied myself with working at a nonprofit, studying for my Master's degree in biotechnology, and attending everyone's wedding but my own. Would I end up an old maid, or worse yet, would I fall for someone my parents wouldn't accept and then be cast out of our family?

I met Ali on a Sunday afternoon in mid-January when his cousin brought him over for an "initial" visit. My mom informed me literally an hour before their arrival, and she picked out my clothes and mismatched jewelry in between cooking a variety of dishes in a frenzy. After hearing the doorbell, I hid in the office, playing solitaire on the computer to calm my nerves while my parents chitchatted with him in the living room. As I heard them walk down the hall, I had little choice but to emerge from my hiding spot. I stood face-to-face with a tall, clean-shaven, middle-parted-hair beanpole. We sat on opposite ends of the room and exchanged nothing more than surreptitious glances.

After the lunch feast, my dad practically forced me to follow Ali into the dining area, where I could hear him whistling to my lovebirds and trying to get them to touch his fingers through the cage. *Cute.* When he saw me, he pulled out a chair and motioned for me to sit. He leaned back and stretched his long legs out in front of him, totally at ease. I sat on the edge of my chair, unsure what to say, feeling as if I was in a job interview, a permanent one. But his questions were uncomplicated, his tone friendly, sparking through shared interests in music and nature. I sensed something that I could not pinpoint. Maybe it was an immediate comfort in sitting face-to-face, or his relaxed demeanor, or his cute dimples when he smiled, which was often. We exchanged email addresses when it was time for him to go.

After that meeting, we spent countless hours writing to each other, covering the basics like hobbies, education, religion, and future aspirations. Ali's emails were warm and funny, respectful yet so casual that I felt as if we had been friends for years. And then I told him about my autoimmune disease, anxious that he would disappear as others before had done. His response was unexpected.

"I just read your email and admire your braveness and frankness each passing day. We all have something or the other . . . and I do not make anything of what you have said other than that it has enhanced the respect I have for you, if nothing else."

It was not just an "okay, we can figure this out" or a simple "thanks for sharing this with me," but an all-out affirmation, his words giving me a new confidence. I found myself waking up every morning with a new email in my inbox, only to fall asleep smiling after reading his childhood stories and hiking adventures, and about his love of music and travel.

Two weeks later, on a wintry afternoon, he came for another visit. My parents encouraged us to go on a drive, just the two of us. He sat in the passenger seat, and we drove. Though he was twenty-seven and studying for a doctorate, his boyish face and lanky frame made him look like a teenager. "So where do we go from here?"

"Oh, I thought we were going to DC. Is that okay?" I focused on the highway.

Ali was silent for a second and continued, "No, where do *we* go from here?"

I clutched the steering wheel tighter, my gloved hands suddenly clammy as adrenaline buzzed throughout my body—my mind a jumble of confused thoughts.

I could feel his expressive eyes on me. "I mean, how much more time would you like to decide?" His long, slender fingers playfully tapped the console.

"I'm not sure," I said. "I mean, we've just known each other for two weeks. Don't you need more time?"

"No, not really. My mind is already set."

"I'm not sure," I repeated.

"Okay, take as much time as you need." Ali grinned.

What? Was this his way of proposing? What happened to getting down on one knee? Where were the ring and the flowers in case I said yes?

The rest of the ride to DC was quiet, each of us lost in our own thoughts. His question had been so nonchalant that it felt more like a business deal. He had already signed the contract, but my pen was still afloat in midair.

The following afternoon, Ali sent me an email.

"Hey, Saadia! Would you care to let me watch you as you sleep each night for the rest of your life?

"Too cheeky, I guess . . . I'll come up with a better one later."

Cheeky? I couldn't recall when I had ever heard that word before. And later? *How much later?* And just how did he expect me to respond? *Via email?*

Since when did proposals in arranged marriages take place virtually? I always imagined the parents from both sides sitting in a formal living room, sipping *chai* and nibbling on biscuits. Then, the guy's side asks the girl's side for her hand in marriage to their humble son, followed by jubilant hugs, the soon-to-be bride and groom smiling shyly. At least, that's what I saw in the Pakistani TV serials. No one had ever described their arranged marriage proposals—not my mother, aunts, or older cousins. *What did I know?*

Did I like him enough to say yes? My American side said no; two weeks was just too fast. My Pakistani side said yes, you know him more than you ever could have hoped for before marriage. I was teetering on a scale, my overly analytical mind weighing the pros and cons as if it could be that simple.

And tonight, at the dinner table, my parents jumped off the sidelines just two days after our Sunday drive. "Saadia, why are you taking so long?" my father asked, while I poured my mom's famous chutney onto my plate.

I looked up at him in confusion. *Did he expect me to be done with dinner already?* We had just sat down, and I hadn't even taken a bite.

"About Ali. Why are you taking so long to decide?"

My spoon froze in midair.

"Saadia, is there any problem with him?" my mother asked, and then took a bite of naan. *How can she eat while asking me the most important question of my life?*

"Uh, no, no problem," I stammered, feeling the blood rush to my face.

Dad continued the interrogation. "So then, why not say yes?" I felt as if he could see through me, as if he knew I wanted to say yes but didn't have the nerve. I didn't even know the basics. Was he organized? Did he leave his socks on the floor? Was he a couch potato? Did he like to go out?

"What's the hurry though?" I asked, feeling sweat on my forehead.

"Saadia? What is it? What's bothering you?" Dad asked gently, his hands resting by the sides of his plate.

"Nothing." *Yet everything.* I couldn't pinpoint any problem.

"I think he's a good boy, educated, with a great personality, jolly." My mom—in fact, both of my parents—really loved that he was "jolly." It came up in every conversation I had with them. But didn't I love that about him, too? His genuine humor, his ability to make everyone laugh around him, and his easy smile?

"Yes, he is." I moved my spoon slowly around the grains of rice. I felt like I was in a movie, except someone had pressed the fast-forward button, and everything was flying at superspeed.

"So then? Do you want to say yes?" Mom was on the edge of her chair, her legs in position to leap.

I paused briefly; Ali's image floated in front of my eyes. His handsome face, the way he cocked his head to make sure he caught my every word.

"Okay." That's all I could muster. I nodded and smiled shyly, my heart suddenly pounding and pumping faster and faster, as if I was sitting on the front seat of a roller coaster on the verge of plummeting straight down. *What did I just do?* There was silence. I stared down, too. An eternity passed before my parents grinned, my father rising from his chair.

Twenty years and three kids later, as my father had predicted, "This is the best decision you'll ever make."

Vacation

Jeniffer Thompson

It was 1979—a devilishly cold winter in northern Idaho. I was nine, Lilli was five, and Julie was a baby. My daddy, a restless man at heart, was itchin' to head south. "Get some sun." He'd met a new friend at the local tavern the night before. They were swapping bear stories when Ron announced his plan to drive his fancy RV to New Mexico to visit family for Christmas. It didn't take long before Daddy had hitched himself to that plan.

"We'll go along with 'em, split the gas, make a family vacation of it."

Mom didn't want to go. The idea of spending Christmas in a motorhome with strangers didn't sound appealing, but he talked her into it.

I'll tell you what, though; that RV was a sight to behold. It even had sleeping compartments, more than we girls had at home. We were used to sleeping on the living room fold-out. Plus, it had a nicer kitchen than ours. Bigger, too—it even had running water and a working toilet.

Rolling along in that fancy rig made me feel pretty fancy myself.

They had two boys: Jimmy, twelve, and Beau, eight. Jimmy had bronzed skin, dreamy dark eyes, and shiny black hair that he wore in a long ponytail. He usually had his head in a book, which didn't leave much opportunity to start up any idle conversation, but I had time on my side. The drive to Taos Pueblo from our spot in the middle of nowhere, Idaho, would take twenty-two hours if we drove straight through.

Well, things turned sideways right quick. To begin with, the younger boy, Beau, decided he had a crush on me, and he kept hovering around me singing that Robert Palmer song "Bad Case of Loving You (Doctor, Doctor)." I can still hear him singing about how he loved me. Yuck. Lilli thought it was hysterical. As you can imagine, it got on my nerves after about six hours, and I think the adults must have been annoyed, too, because they started arguing.

"What's the sense in that?" I heard Daddy say, over the humming of that big motor.

"Steven, we're goin' my way."

Mr. Treetop didn't want to dilly-dally. Daddy wanted to take it slow. He'd been telling Mr. Treetop all about the US Interstate Highway System and the fence-building techniques that linked farmer to farmer across "this beautiful country."

Daddy loved educatin' people. "Now, listen," Daddy said. "If we cut down through Idaho and into the plains of Utah—the rock formations there are a sight to behold, my friend. And, if we dip into Arizona, I can show you a perfect ruby the size of my thumb. It's a place that only I know about, ya see. A ruby so big—yes, sir—if I had the right tools and a few days, I'd be a rich man. I'd be willing to share it with you, too, friend."

Mr. Treetop continued to stare straight ahead on I-90 as we passed the I-15.

"You missed it! You passed right on by."

"We ain't got time for that. I told ya—we're goin' my way."

"Well, you ain't got no sense, friend," Daddy said. "Why would you own a monstrous vehicle like this if you had no intention of using it for its intended purpose?"

"Eh?!" Mr. Treetop jerked the wheel, sending our Chutes and Ladders board right off the table with a crash. "This is my trip." He straightened the wheel and pulled us back into a straight line. "You'll be happy with whatever we do."

"The hell I will!"

"If you don't like it, you and yours can get out and walk. I'll pull over right here." Mr. Treetop made like he was getting ready to pull over. Mom gripped Julie in her arms, and Lilli and I looked at each other in horror. That shut Daddy up.

A simmering silence filled the space. I looked over at Jimmy, and you know what? He was grinning at me with steely-cold eyes, enjoying this. My heart sank. The boy I loved was happy to leave me on the side of the road. I guess that was my first heartbreak.

For the next ten hours, Beau continued to sing at me, but he wasn't crushin', cause the lyrics turned sinister. The boys took to lashing Lilli and me with paper-cut-thin whispers that they floated over us as they passed by. "Ugly. We're gonna leave you out in the cold to die."

I could not wait to get loosed from that forty-five-foot rolling beast—the fanciness had completely worn off. By the time we reached Taos Pueblo and the Treetops' family home, the temperature inside the RV was icy. They agreed that we would sleep in the RV while the Treetops slept in the house. Daddy tipped his hat in his amiable way, thanking Mr. Treetop for his hospitality, smiling broadly as they walked their luggage off the RV.

The next day, Daddy looked into getting us bus tickets home, but he didn't have enough money.

"We'll just have to keep an eye on Ron. He won't leave till after Christmas, so we just need to make sure we're in the RV when they're settin' to head out." Mr. Treetop and his family loaded into the RV the day after Christmas. It didn't take but ten miles before the boys started in on their tormenting. They didn't even bother hiding it from the adults anymore.

Daddy and Mr. Treetop argued over everything, but after a while, the arguing stopped altogether and the adults were silent, which was somehow worse than the arguing.

Daddy wouldn't let any of us get out whenever we stopped for gas. The farther north we drove, the worse things got—storms were brewing inside and out. The next time they stopped, the Treetops all piled off. Jimmy smiled at me. "Aren't you coming? Afraid we're gonna leave you behind?"

As soon as the door closed, Daddy pulled a shotgun out from beneath some blankets and started to load it. Mom flitted about opening drawers and muttering to herself, "There's gotta be some rope around here somewhere."

"Look in the cabinet behind the driver's seat," Daddy hollered.

"Good idea." She reached in, pulled out a long piece of rope, and turned to Daddy. "This should work." She walked back over and handed him the rope. They continued scheming and whisperin'. I wanted to walk back there to hear them better, but I knew to stay put.

"They damn well will drive us home," he said, loudly enough for me to hear. I looked over at Lilli, whose eyes were wide. I put my arm around her just as Daddy bellowed out, "with a shotgun at their necks." I squeezed Lilli tighter. Then, I heard Mom say, "I'll tie *him* up first," before her voice trailed off, and they started whispering again.

Daddy placed the gun back under the blanket just as the Treetops piled back onto the RV. I tried to avoid eye contact with Jimmy. His eyes revealed everything. Like, he didn't care if I lived or died, and he might actually prefer it *if I did die.*

"You girls want to play Go Fish?" Mom asked us.

"No," we answered back in unison.

I could feel the wheels rolling beneath us as I stared out the window and counted the mile markers as I drifted off to sleep. It was early the next morning when I woke up to see a landscape that I recognized. The trees were taller and denser, the snow banks were thicker, and Diamond Lake was coming into view. We were twenty miles from home. Thick snowflakes danced around us, threatening to whip up a storm.

"Just let 'em out here," one of the boys said. "Come on, Dad, don't drive 'em, they can hitchhike."

I looked over at Daddy, whose eyes were like slits of dark glass that stared straight ahead, his arms concealed under a blanket that was laid out across his lap. I was expecting him to jump up with that shotgun and make them all get off so we could drive ourselves home. Mr. Treetop ignored his boys. It turns out they had made a deal. Daddy had promised to pay him $500 if he delivered us home safely. The RV rolled to a stop in front of our little house. Daddy opened the RV door and we were greeted with the kind of silence you only get after a heavy snowfall.

Once safely inside, Daddy took to loading wood into the stove as Mom handed baby Julie to me and wrapped us girls in a blanket. Soon enough, the fire was roaring and Mom got to making a batch of sugar cookies. It seemed like an hour had passed and yet I could still hear that RV idling outside.

Pretty soon, I was startled by the sound of footsteps on the porch and a rap on the door.

Daddy answered it as if an old friend had come to visit. "Well, hello there, Ron. What can I do you for?"

Mr. Treetop stood there, dumbstruck.

After a few seconds of silence, he knew Daddy wasn't going to pay him that $500. He turned around, defeated, and trudged on back to the RV. It was snowing again. Large fluffy snowflakes collected on his slumped shoulders as he walked.

Daddy called out to him as he stepped up into the RV, "Ya'll drive carefully, now, ya hear? Those roads are liable to be slick as snot." I liked watching that man walk away. He'd finally wrestled with the wrong bear.

Anchoring

Lauren Woolley

February 2013

"You're transgender?"

My husband looks up slowly and tearfully. "Yes." Then, he cradles his head and sobs.

My heart races and my head weighs a million pounds. The dining room spins. I grab a chair to stabilize myself. I gulp for air, but it's like breathing through a straw. *Get a grip . . . Keep it together . . . breathe in . . . breathe ouuut . . . breathe in . . . breathe ouuut . . . breathe in . . . breathe ouuut.* Slowly, my brain releases a stream of emotional anesthesia. The room eases to a stop. I see the vase of pink gerbera daisies on the table. I notice the wrought-iron tiles hanging on the wall. I painted them silver to match our chandelier. I comprehend my husband's words, but my mind has no folder in which to file them. My life just radically changed. His brown eyes look up at me. He wipes away tears in between hitching breaths. My heart draws me into its deepest chambers. However, I quickly scramble out. I take shelter in my head because it's safer here.

My psychologist-self starts steering the ship. Stormy seas don't scare her. She can take a wave of fear, let it wash over her, and pull someone out of a crisis. *But wait, this crisis involves me.*

I slide out of the chair and join my husband. I inhale deeply and press my feet firmly into the floor. I have a job to do. I struggle with which pronoun to use. I had referred to my husband for eight years as "he." The world assigned my best friend a gender that does not fit.

I lean forward, listen, and nod. My psychologist-self interacts with my husband while the rest of me struggles in the surf. It's hard to follow the conversation underneath the waves. *How did we get here?*

Throughout our relationship, my husband's gender identity was like a leak in the basement. I heard dripping, but I ignored it. I panicked when he first told me he enjoyed wearing women's clothing. Then, I got curious. My research revealed that gender expression lives on a spectrum, versus a pink or blue box. No one batted an eye when I wore my boyfriend's bomber jacket. Why should I care that my husband likes to wear mini-skirts? I specifically asked him if he was transgender. He said, "No, I'm a heterosexual guy who likes to cross-dress." I think we both wanted to believe this story.

On the surface, our life sparkled: a home in San Diego, good jobs, and the love of Buddy, our rescue pup. Over several years, I witnessed my husband's depression roll in like a fog while his closet, full of dresses, skirts, and heels, received minimal attention. I heard the *plunk, plunk, plunk* of the drops in the basement. *Why bother going down there?* We can keep walking our dog, riding our bikes, and meeting up with friends.

When I felt the water seeping underneath the door, my husband grew distant. He came home late tonight and snapped at me when I asked about his whereabouts. Now, water gushes into our home, and we scramble for safety.

In between my husband's sobs, I remember hearing, "I'm sorry . . . I can move to an extended-stay hotel . . . we'll need to sell the condo . . . you'll have to keep Buddy since he can't stay in a hotel . . . I'll have to talk to HR . . . we'll have to figure out the divorce." Hot tears sting my cheeks and a lump forms in my throat. I croak out, "OK, let's just take this one step at a time. I want you to be happy. It's late. We both have work tomorrow. Let's go to bed and keep talking about it tomorrow."

"OK."

We hug each other tightly. I haul my sluggish body up the stairs. I shove my husband's truth into the back of my emotional closet, slam the door, and go to bed. I lay next to my husband. Someone I know well. Someone I really don't know at all. Miraculously, I fall asleep. I wake up, go to work, and return to an empty home. Then, I lose it.

I slump onto the bottom stairs. I try moving, but gravity holds me firmly in place. My new reality rips my heart to shreds. *My marriage is ending. The man I know is gone.* I hug my knees to my chest and rock back and forth. Then, my brain simply unplugs from its emotional center. Time stands still. I feel no pain. I float above and watch a thirty-seven-year-old woman fall apart. It's quiet up here. I want to stay here, but Buddy's head, nuzzling my leg, snaps me back into reality.

I wipe my eyes and nose with my sleeve. Traces of mascara, foundation, and lipstick now decorate the cuffs. I am drowning. The riptide will drag me to sea if I do not reach out. I need an anchor. Someone who will not question or judge me. Someone who will hold their own shock and not pour it back on me. *Everyone thinks we are happily married. No one will see this coming.* I need someone to simply hold a bucket for my tears and not complain when it gets heavy. I need my sister.

I grab the strap of my purse and haul it into my lap. I rummage for my phone. My hands shake as I dial. It reminds me of those anxious dreams in which I need emergency help, but my fingers hit the wrong buttons. I take a deep breath and steady myself. My sister says hello, and my throat constricts. I squeak out, "Something happened. We are getting a divorce. I need to see you."

No judgment or questions from my sister.

"Come. Just come," she says.

I find a cheap flight that departs the next day. This thin thread keeps me tethered to my life raft. The hard landing at Washington Reagan jolts me awake from my red-eye flight. I look out the window and see the sun rising over the Potomac River. I am usually the lone passenger up with the reading light. However, my exhausted body has slept for the duration of the flight. After disembarking, I walk straight into the bathroom. I splash water on my face. I hope it's the horrid fluorescent lighting that makes me look like a zombie. *Who is this woman?*

I plod through the terminal. My suitcase wheels skip the seams in the linoleum: bump, bump, bump. I pinch the bridge of my nose in hopes of containing my tears. I see a large crowd waiting in the loading zone. I take deep breaths because the heat of my tears fills my throat and eyes. Warm drops roll down my cheeks. *Maybe people will think that I'm here for a funeral.* In some ways, I did just experience a death.

I emit a sigh of relief when my sister's black Prius sides up to the curb. I toss my suitcase in the trunk, hop into the passenger seat, and close the door. She grabs my hand and looks at me, tears forming in the corners of her eyes.

"He's, I mean, she's transgender. We're getting a divorce because she's transgender."

My sister does not flinch. "I'm so sorry."

"I feel like I'm going to die."

"I know. You can do this. I'm going to be right here with you."

I release my breath and sink into the passenger seat. My boat is now firmly moored to an anchor. The sea may toss and jolt me, but I will not drown.

7.9 Seconds

Mary-Jean Zampino

Seven-point-nine seconds—that's how quickly it happened. Not eight seconds, but rather seven-point-nine, to be exact. At least, that's what the police report indicated when it was translated from German to English. It's just like the Germans to be so damn precise. But even with a brutally graphic description of the scene, I wasn't sure my brothers and I would ever understand what happened the night we became orphans.

My parents and I had only been in Stuttgart for three months. My father had accepted a promotion as the new European sales manager, and our stay was supposed to last three years. For him, this promotion was a long-overdue acknowledgment of hard work. For my mother, it was a dream come true. We would have the chance to travel to Paris to explore the world of fashion or to southern Italy to visit our extended family. For me, a seventeen-year-old entering my senior year of high school, it was a nightmare.

It was August 1981, and I was distraught at the idea of leaving my hometown in Connecticut. I had lived all my life in the same house and had known my circle of friends since I was five. Once we'd made it to Germany, I would have to attend a military school because it was the only place that taught classes in English. This was important, given my German was limited to "danke schoen" (thank you, Wayne Newton) and "gesundheit."

"You may not be able to see it now, but once we get to Europe, you'll understand. We'll get to see the beautiful cathedrals of Fatima and Notre Dame, walk through the remains of war-damaged cities, and even see the *Mona Lisa* firsthand. It will broaden your horizons!"

"*You* love history, Mom; I don't. And my horizons are just fine the size they are—no broadening needed."

But there was no winning this fight. My three brothers were all in college or working, so they wouldn't be moving with us. I was the youngest, the only girl. So, four days after my seventeenth birthday, we flew to our new home in Stuttgart, West Germany.

Within a few months, I was surprised to find that I felt at home in the impeccably clean streets and among the old-world Tudor-style architecture. Some of the houses looked just like they came out of the pages of a real-life Grimms' fairy tale. It helped that almost everyone spoke English, and I was proud to pick up a few new German words here and there, like the day my neighbor's toddler taught me the word "scheisse."

What surprised me was that, for the first time in my life, my parents and I were on the same level. Back home, my parents were the authorities on life. In Germany, we were learning and experiencing things for the first time together. We tried lebkuchen, a delicious gingerbread pastry. We discovered new smells, like the juicy bratwurst on the street corners; we learned to say "tschüss"—a way of casually saying "see you later."

On Friday, October 30, my mother was excited to tell me, "Hartmut, from your father's office, thought it would be nice if they cooked a traditional German meal at their home tonight, and you are invited." I could see the delight in my mother's eyes, but I had other plans.

"But tonight, we're gonna decorate the gym for tomorrow's homecoming dance. A couple of my new friends invited me."

It hadn't been easy to fit in at the military school, but homecoming was an opportunity to make new friends. On the other hand, after hearing the stories about the characters in my father's office, I was curious to meet his coworkers.

"Well, it's up to you, honey. Just give me a call from school if you're going to stay, so we know when and where we should pick you up."

By the afternoon, my decision had been made. My new friends had talked me into joining them in decorating the gym, followed by the treat of a bonfire. I made my way to the phone booth on campus and called my mom. "Dad will have other business dinners, right? There's only one homecoming. I feel like I should go; then, maybe I'll get invited to other events."

"That's fine, honey, and yes, there will be other dinners. What time shall we get you?"

"10:30 p.m." I told her I would be ready and waiting in front of the school entrance. We did our typical hanging-up routine.

"Love you, Mom."

"Love you, too, honey. We'll see you later tonight."

"Tschüss," I said.

"Tschüss," she said.

My mom had a thing about never hanging up angry.

"Mary-Jean, don't ever hang up angry with anyone," she would say. "You never know when that might just be your last conversation."

After the bonfire, everyone went home. I sat on the benches outside the school entrance with my new friend Earl. But my parents didn't show up. I kept it light. "My parents are infamously late. And think about it, they don't speak German, my dad is still learning the roads, and they've only been to the school a few times. I'm guessing they're lost. And now that it's starting to rain, it's probably making it harder for them to see."

But soon 11:30 p.m. came, and then 12:30 a.m., and 1:30 a.m. I was dying of embarrassment and shivering in the rain. How could my parents do this to me, much less in front of my new friend? Finally, at 2:30 a.m., soaked to the bone, Earl turned to me. "Umm, I don't think your parents are coming; why don't you call them from my house?" When we got to his house, Earl's stepfather was not happy that we had woken him up. I called my parents twice, but no one answered.

"Well, you can't stay here. Let me call the military police to take you home," Earl's stepfather said. Within ten minutes, a young soldier showed up in his Jeep; Earl and I said our goodbyes. The soldier seemed pleased to be fulfilling the mission of getting the young girl home safely. He tried to make small talk with me during the ride, but I was in no mood. *Why are they always so late?* But the truth was that a sliver of worry was starting to surface. It didn't help that the soldier got lost on the autobahn and overshot our exit by a good twenty minutes. When we finally arrived at the house, it was close to 4:00 a.m.

"I'm sure your parents are okay, and everything will be just fine."

I noticed my dad's company car wasn't parked in the driveway like usual, and I could feel my stomach tighten. The soldier ensured I got in safely, and then he left.

Being raised with manners, I waited until 6:00 a.m. to call my father's coworker, Hartmut, to see if he had any idea what had happened to my parents. He told me that they had left around ten to come pick me up. Worried, he said he would make some calls.

Forty-five minutes later, he called me back.

"Hello, this is Hartmut."

"Hello, Hartmut. Did you find my parents? Are they okay?" There was an eerie silence, and then I heard Hartmut struggling to get the words out.

"Are my parents, okay?" My voice grew louder as I struggled not to throw up.

"I'm so sorry. I'm so very sorry. Your parents were killed in an accident on the way to get you last night."

I dropped the phone, then quickly picked it back up. What did he just say? My parents didn't pick me up because they were killed? They were dead? They weren't coming home? It was as if I was out of my body, hearing the words but not understanding what they meant. I sat down, feeling my body shake. I wouldn't ever see them again? And they left me by myself . . . in this foreign country?

Only minutes earlier, I'd been ready to call them out for deserting me at school. Now, I'd never get to see them, or hug them, again. I thought of the softness of my mother's skin as I hugged her goodbye that morning.

I was in shock. Of all the hypothetical scenarios I ran by Earl, my parents being killed was not one that crossed my mind. I didn't know how to process this information, so I just did what my parents had always taught me: I thanked Hartmut for calling me. Yeah, I actually *thanked* him.

A lot of things can happen in seven-point-nine seconds. You can take a bite of a gingerbread pastry, smell the juicy bratwurst on the street corners, or learn how to say "tschüss." These are things I would never be able to do with my parents again because of those seven-point-nine seconds on a rainy night in Stuttgart, West Germany.

ABOUT THE EDITORS

MARNI FREEDMAN

Marni Freedman is a screenwriter, playwright, award-winning author, writing coach, and co-founder and executive director for the San Diego Writers Festival. She leads the Memoir Certificate Program for San Diego Writers, Ink, is the executive producer of the International Memoir Writers Association's theatrical Memoir Showcase, and co-edits *Shaking the Tree: brazen. short. memoir.* You can find Marni at MarniFreedman.com, a hub to help writers find their authentic voice. Her latest book, *How to Unblock and Become a Creative Force of Nature: A Mindful Approach to Artistic Badassery,* will be published in 2026 by Hay House.

TRACY J. JONES

Tracy J. Jones is a professional content writer, developmental editor, and writing coach. She is the co-producer, head judge, writing coach, and co-director of the Memoir Showcase. She co-edits the award-winning Memoir Showcase anthology, *Shaking the Tree: brazen. short. memoir.* She is a co-instructor for the year-long Memoir Certificate program at San Diego Writers, Ink, and runs three writing groups. She is the president and a founding board member of the International Writers Association. She is the Warwick's + San Diego Writers Festival Book Club interviewer. She can be reached at tracyjoneseditor@gmail.com.

SPECIAL THANKS

Caroline Gilman for our beautiful cover and overall design; Erin Willard for copy editing the manuscript; and the entire International Memoir Writers Association for supporting this project and the San Diego Writers Festival. The IMWA Board: Marni Freedman, Tracy J. Jones, Caroline Gilman, Anastasia Zadeik, Saadia Esmail, Leslie Ferguson, Jane Muschenetz, Robert Kirk Donaldson, Lenore Greiner, Holly Kammier, Shiloh Rasmussen, and Janet Hafner.

An additional thank you to our donors and angel supporters who have allowed these stories to be shared with our larger memoir community.

www.ingramcontent.com/pod-product-compliance
Ingram Content Group UK Ltd.
Pitfield, Milton Keynes, MK11 3LW, UK
UKHW031317310125
4392UKWH00035B/391

9 798218 563509